Called From Lebanon

Called From Lebanon

A Memoir by
Marie Bond

For information:

Twin Cedars Books

Production and creative:

jonathangullery.design@gmail.com

FIRST EDITION

ISBN Print: 979-8-9867985-0-9

ISBN Ebook: 979-8-9867985-1-6

Printed in the United States of America

Contents

Preface

Every person has a story to tell, and every person's life story is worth telling. All the experiences we go through, the challenges that we face, the choices that we make, and the path that we take leave a mark on someone's heart. Each life is a continuity of all the lives that came before it.

Love is everlasting because that's what we take with us for eternity. The love of parents, the love of children, the love of husband and wife, the love of siblings, neighbors, and friends, and all the kinds of love that we experience are engraved in our memory and in our soul for all time. Love transcends life and accompanies us forever.

This is my story and testimony. I don't want to mention anything that was hurtful, or condemn any person who hurt me. God is love, and He loves everyone the same. Our behavior affects ourselves more than it affects others. And when we do something good for others, we are the ones who enjoy it the most.

I was born in a beautiful country, Lebanon, and I was raised surrounded by many cousins and relatives as well as neighbors and friends. I was 15 years old when civil war started in Lebanon, but God protected me and shielded me from all harm. I am here today to testify about His love and to return my gratitude.

I met a young man named Adel, who introduced me to an ideal that any person in any place can connect to—the ideal of a family centered upon God— and a blueprint for building this ideal that involves overcoming the differences that separate people from each other and working together to build a world of peace through establishing peaceful families.

Jesus said "You will know them by their fruit" (Matthew 7:16). I worked with people who truly lived for others. There was no other platform that brought Christians, Muslims, Buddhists, and people of other religions to work together harmoniously for peace. There was no other platform which attracted youth to build families centered upon God's ideal and principles. My soul, my conscience, and my heart showed me the way. If it was false, I would have known before anyone else. But it was the right path, and it was the true ideal.

The truth is that every person should realize that he or she is God's precious child and that every couple is a parental figure, representing God's parental love not only to their own children but also to their own community and relatives. Each one of us should try to substantiate God's ideal in our life as a child, a spouse, and a parent.

I hope that my story can inspire everyone who reads it. The purpose of writing it is to show how God has worked through my life and how I found through my own dreams and personal experiences the true value of this ideal.

I realized that it's really not only my story; it's my ancestors, my parents, my spiritual parents, and the whole community who prepared the way for me. It is, most of all, the story of God's absolute love for me. Because of His love I am blessed and forever grateful.

Amen

ONE

My Country

Let me begin my story by introducing my country, Lebanon. It is a small country in the Middle East, a land of 4,000 square miles, with the highest mountain peak at around 10,000 feet above sea level. The Mediterranean Sea is on its west, Syria on its north and east, and Israel on its south.

The country enjoys a Mediterranean climate. Summer is hot and humid while winter is cold and rainy. The temperature can drop below freezing in the mountains so there is a lot of snow.

Forests cover around 13% of the land. There is a wide range of trees, from pine to wild almond, juniper, fir, and oak trees. In ancient times, Lebanon was covered by a large forest of cedar trees, the national emblem of the country. Now only a few remain, due to constant threat from wild-fires caused by long dry summer seasons.

While many of its surrounding countries are desert lands, Lebanon produces all kinds of fruit trees, from apples and peaches to oranges and lemons. The agriculture sector employs 12% of its total workforce.

Lebanon's early civilization dates back more than five thousand years. It was the home of the Phoenicians, whose maritime culture flourished for thousands of years.

Lebanon used to be known as the Switzerland of the Middle East, famous for its tourism, agriculture, commerce, and banking. It was a destination for the Arabs and the Europeans to enjoy summer swimming in its warm Mediterranean Sea and in winter to ski in its snowy mountains. But things changed. Since the Palestinians started fleeing to Lebanon due to the Arab-Israeli war beginning in 1948, the country became overwhelmed by refugees seeking shelter.

In 1975, a cycle of violence between the Palestinian refugees and the Lebanese militias started in Beirut. The country was divided between the Christians, who were worried about the Palestinian guerillas fighting Israel from Lebanon, and the Muslims, supported by the Arabs, who were sympathizing with the Palestinian cause and their right to fight against Israel even at the cost of the Lebanese people.

The conflict escalated and became a civil war, which continued until 1990, when other countries like Syria and Israel got involved. It was literally the war of others in our land. Over 120,000 people were killed, and thousands were injured. It devastated the economy and since then Lebanon never recovered, despite all efforts at revival. So many patriots gave their lives and so many leaders were assassinated. The country became ruled by corruption and an unqualified government.

Because Lebanon never had border laws banning people from entering the country without documentation, in 2011, following the outbreak of the Syrian civil war, Syrian refugees began entering Lebanon in large numbers. It was estimated that Lebanon received over one million Syrian refugees between 2011 and 2016, on top of the Palestinian refugees from the past. This led to destruction of the country's economy and infrastructure.

Lebanon and its people continue to suffer endlessly as the unresolved Arab-Israeli conflict continues

My Family

I was born in Beirut in 1960, the eldest of three children, me and my two brothers, Ibrahim and Fadi.My father, Elias Akiki, was a clerk and collector working for a famous French-language weekly publication named *L'Hebdo Magazine* or more commonly *Magazine,* which was owned by Georges Abou Adal. He worked there for 25 years. After he retired, he worked for Jean Claude Boulos, a famous TV host who managed a marketing company.

He was the only son in his family, with five sisters. His father worked at a café in downtown Beirut where men gathered to play backgammon (tawlé), one of the oldest two-person board games. They smoked hookah (arguilé) and sipped arak, the famous Lebanese alcohol. So, from an early age, my father was introduced to smoking and drinking while he was helping his father in the cafe and enjoying the social setting.

In his teenage years, he worked selling tickets at movie theaters. It was an opportunity for him to watch all kinds of western movies which helped him to learn English. But the highlight of my father's youth was being an accomplished swimmer. Summer or winter, rain or shine, he used to go to the beach. Swimming was his lifelong hobby.

One of the stories that my grandma told us was that one day when my father went swimming, a sudden strong wave emerged and took him very far from the shore. He tried very hard to swim back but the waves were very high and his friends could not help him. He started losing his strength and losing hope when suddenly he saw a big rock that he clung to for over an hour until he got help. His body was covered with cuts and scratches that left their scars.

As a bachelor going into his thirties, after his father had passed away and his mother was getting old, his sisters started worrying about him and pushing him to get married. They even asked their church pastor to find him a good wife. Abouna Boutros, the pastor, took the request seriously endeavored to find a good wife for my father.

My mother, Hélené Abou Karam, the youngest of six children, with two brothers and three sisters, was born in Baskinta, a village which is just over 26 miles from Beirut. She came from a family known for its generosity and help to others. Her father was a landlord and a salesman. In the early 1900s, he decided to sell some of his land and take a trip to America, the land of opportunity, seeking a better life for his family. It took him six months by sea to arrive in New York. He tried to do business selling various items but, unfortunately, he did not succeed. It was harder than he expected so he returned home.

When her father passed away, as she was the only one who was still single, my mother moved in with her eldest brother and his family. Her mother went to live with her second son. My mother received a lot of marriage proposals, mostly from the men in the village, but she kept refusing them. She did not want to stay in the village. She had always dreamed of traveling and visiting new places.

As Abouna Boutros hometown was from a nearby village to my mom's, and because everyone knows everyone in the village, he went and visited her. In the beginning, my mother hesitated and she was not interested. But her brother and his family encouraged her to accept my father as a good candidate after they found out that he had a good job, he lived in the city, and he had a good reputation as an honest man.

When my parents got married, my paternal grandmother lived with them. In the Middle East, the son is the one who takes care of and provides for his old parents. So, despite my father having five sisters, my mother was the one who took care of her mother-in-law until she passed away.

I never knew my grandfathers; both of them died before I was born. But I heard a lot of stories about them from my parents and from my grandmothers. My mother used to tell us how her father was always inviting his neighbors and friends to come and eat with him. It was hard on my grandma because she always needed to cook extra to feed anyone passing by. Another story that my aunt told me about my paternal grandfather was that after he passed away, he came to visit my grandmother every Friday in her dreams. They were very close to each other. And what is interesting is that, although I had never met him before, I saw him once in my dream coming to see me. He must be very active spiritually.

My Childhood

My father was a good man. He worked very hard for over forty years and was known for his honesty and loyalty. But he had a bad habit of drinking and smoking. Although he never harmed anyone and rarely became drunk, this kind of life brought a heavy atmosphere to our home and hurt my mother tremendously. No one in her family drank or smoked other than on special occasions. And because my father was the only son, my aunts used to come to visit very often and stay for lunch or dinner. They also used to socialize with my father, drinking and enjoying happy hours. I always remember my mother during the holidays spending most of the time in the kitchen cooking and preparing for her sisters-in-law and their families. That wasn't the kind of life that she dreamed about. Nevertheless, she endured and persevered because there was no other alternative for her. Marriage is for life, through good and bad.

My parents were devoted Catholics. They attended mass every Sunday, but they didn't impose on me and my brothers any obligations or any beliefs. It was just natural to attend the church on Sundays and on holidays. We were baptized and received holy communion as part of growing up as Catholics. Both my parents had strong faith and a strong prayer life. I remember seeing my father every night devoting time to pray with a sincere heart. And later, when my parents became older, they started praying together. Every night, both of them went to their room, lit a candle in front of Saint Mary and Jesus' picture, and said their prayers.

Growing up surrounded by so many relatives helped me to become a social person and to relate to people with confidence. We had more than thirty direct cousins, but we grew up mostly with ten of them who were my uncles' children and who were our age. Although at that time we didn't appreciate it, my brothers and I received so much love from our aunts. They treated us like a royal family. After all, their dream came true and their only brother got married to a wonderful woman from the village. Everyone acknowledged that my mother was the best addition to their family. Even my grandma used to say that her daughter-in-law was better than her own five daughters.

My favorite time while I was growing up was when we went to Baskinta, my mother's village. Surrounded by pine trees in the hills and fruit trees in the valley, Baskinta lies at the foot of Mount Saninne, where the sun and the moon rise behind this majestic mountain. Every summer, without exception, we packed and left the city to spend three full months in the village. We used to rent a little place there but, because of lack of income for many months due to the war, my parents couldn't afford to continue renting it. My mother decided to clean up her parents' old abandoned house so that we could keep enjoying our summer in the village. Although my grandparents' house needed so much fixing and renovation, as children we didn't mind. We spent most of the day playing outside, often eating in the garden and at picnics with our relatives and neighbors.

I spent the best times of my childhood in Baskinta with my two cousins, Nada and Maguy, and my neighbor, Silva. The four of us enjoyed a deep friendship that continued throughout the years even until now. We went on picnics and took hikes together. We cooked and shared our meals together. We played, we prayed, and even we danced. We were like butterflies, happy and free. The four of us enjoyed a deep friendship that continued throughout the years even until now.

The beauty and the serenity of my village made a strong impact on my childhood. Besides, the village was a safe escape for our family from the horrors of the war. Every time the fighting started in Beirut, we escaped to the village. It was like moving to another country where we felt peaceful and safe.

As the only daughter, my parents enrolled me in a Catholic school and put my two brothers in public school, because the private schools were costly and they could not afford to put all of us there. I was very interested in literature and writing poems. I remember each time that we celebrated a holiday, I wrote a poem for the occasion and proudly recited it in front of my teachers and my classmates. In my senior year, our school participated in a competition to write an essay about the famous Lebanese author Michel Chiha. I entered the contest and won third place representing my school. The former President of Lebanon, Mr. Charles Helou, presented the awards and the ceremony was covered by the National TV. After that, I decided to major in Journalism and Mass Communication. I attended the Lebanese State University for four years and graduated with a bachelor's degree in Journalism.

The two things that I will always miss in my life are my mom and my village. Both of them shaped me to be the person I am today. Both of them were symbols of freedom, trust, love, and beauty. I will always carry with me my mother's love and the best memories from my village for the rest of my life.

TWO

A Decisive Moment

One Christmas evening in1980, someone knocked on my door unexpectedly. My parents were watching TV in the living room, so I went and opened the door. A young man was standing there holding a few Christmas cards in his hand.

"Hello, my name is Adel. I am selling these Christmas cards. Would you like to take a look?"

This was a big surprise, because normally we did not have people selling their goods door to door, especially during war time. Besides, as we were living in an old building on the third floor without an elevator, I was surprised that anyone would climb so many stairs just to sell simple Christmas cards! "This young man must have a strong faith," I said to myself. I invited him to come in, but he hesitated, and when I insisted he agreed to stay for a short time. I offered him a cup of tea and I bought a few cards from him. "Do you by any chance belong to some organization," I asked. Adel replied, "Actually, yes." "May I know the name?" He replied, "Holy Spirit Association for the Unification of World Christianity." "Wow, that must be an important organization. Could you please tell me about it?" "Sure, but not today." And he promised to come again. This encounter would turn out to be a decisive moment in my life.

A few months passed without any sign of him. I was sure that he had forgotten. After all, he was knocking on so many doors. Well, I was wrong. He did come back and this time he brought with him another young man named Alfred. Then Sabah joined them for the following visit. Those three young men, who called each other brothers, started coming to our house very often.

The interesting thing was that my parents did not mind. On the contrary, they enjoyed having them and my mother was happy to cook dinner for them. As our friendship developed, Adel started bringing his guitar and the young men sang for us beautiful French and English songs as well Christian hymns. The atmosphere in our house changed dramatically and became so full of life and full of positive energy that even my neighbors started wondering about those young men.

We went for a picnic and I invited my high school friend, Josephine, to come with us. We brought food to share and we sang and played games. In time, we started discussing deeper topics like the meaning of our lives and why, if God exists, do we have wars and people are suffering?

Adel began sharing with us about the principles and values that he had discovered through the teachings of Rev. Sun Myung Moon, a religious man from Korea, and how this truth changed his perspective on life. So, we started listening to these lectures once a week every time we got together. What is interesting about that time was the unity of heart between those young men. I truly felt that God was among them and that He was trying to reveal Himself to me. It was my personal feeling and experience every time we got together.

In my early twenties, I was truly searching for a high ideal in my life. I was searching for God. I remember that I used to tell God every time on my birthday that there was no meaning for my life unless I did something for Him. Although I used to attend the Catholic church every Sunday and I took catechism at school studying the Bible, somehow I was not content and a lot of questions had no answers. So, when I met Adel and his friends, I felt strongly that their faith was very deep and that they truly applied their beliefs in their daily life. It was not about theories and traditions but mostly it was about God's heart and His utmost desire for humanity to come back to Him and to live in harmony and peace.

Lebanon at that time was in the middle of a civil war. There would be a few months of ceasefire and then a few months of fighting. Because of that unstable and dangerous situation in the country, feeling trapped and not being able to function properly, Adel and his friends would often escape to France and join the movement activities there. Then I would not see them for many months and sometimes even for a year.

They were connected to France because the first missionary who came to Lebanon was from France. Remi Blanchard came to Lebanon in December 1969 and stayed for almost five years. Many young men eventually joined him, including Adel. The first brother who joined him was Sami Ez Eldin, who came from a Druze background.

It was very interesting to learn how a missionary from Germany, Reiner Vincenz, went to France and then a French missionary, Remi

Blanchard, came to Lebanon. The life of a missionary was fascinating to me because I always felt that God sent his missionaries to find the people who were looking for Him, and I was one of them.

While the brothers were in and out of Lebanon, I enrolled in college to study journalism. And every time the fighting started again, I escaped with my family to the village until the city regained its peace. Because of this unpredictable situation in Lebanon, months could pass without my seeing Adel or any other members.

Meeting Vera

My first day in college, during orientation, I met Vera Sawaya. She was with her sister Sona when they approached me. I found out that she grew up in Dhour El Choueir, my uncle's wife's village, and her parents might have met my parents on some occasions. Immediately, we started hanging out together and we became good friends.

Vera had two sisters and one young brother. During our third year in college, a tragedy occurred in her family. While they were in the village escaping from the war zone in Beirut, her father went out with his son for a field trip in the mountains and the boy picked up something from the field and put it in his pocket without the father seeing it. When they came back home, it turned out that it was a bomb, which exploded killing the boy instantly. The family was devastated. They had lost their only son who they had tried very hard to protect and keep safe.

Since that time Vera and I became closer, and we started sharing deeply about the meaning and the purpose of life. I told her about Adel and I shared with her about the Divine Principle values. She was very interested and excited to meet Adel and to know more. Meanwhile, a Japanese couple came to Lebanon as missionaries and rented a first-floor apartment to be used as a public center.

So, when Adel came back, he joined them to live in the center and Vera and I started visiting them often.

Although Vera was the second daughter in her family, she took responsibility as the eldest daughter and started helping her father in his grocery store as well as going to college. As she was the only one who drove at that time, she managed to do a lot of chores for her family and help them to cope with their loss.

In 1984 we graduated together and started looking for jobs. Many of our classmates were already working on national TV or became reporters in famous media outlets. But our path was totally different; God had called us to take a different road than our colleagues.

After knowing Adel for almost four years, I decided to travel with him to Greece to attend a seven-day workshop. At that time, I had come to know Elias and Madeleine Mourad, a married couple who were early members of the movement in Lebanon. In the summer of 1984, I went to Greece together with Madeleine and Adel, and a new chapter in my life began.

Sometimes we wonder how one moment can change our lives, when in truth we were prepared for that moment. I was searching, and God answered my prayers.

THREE

A New Path

In a world where free sex is rampant and individualism is the norm of the society, I was searching for God in my life. A lie can only stay for so long. Everyone has an inner voice which tells them what is right and what is wrong. Our conscience is our best teacher and best educator in guiding us toward what is good and what is bad.

When I attended the seven-day workshop in Greece, I met people from Japan, America, and Europe who came to the Middle East as missionaries. Some of them were working with the *Middle East Times, a newspaper* then based in Cyprus and printed in Athens. Also, I came to meet young people from Turkey, Iran, Sudan, Israel, and Greece. I was impressed by the diversity of the participants. Westerners and Middle Easterners, Christians and Muslims, all gathered under one roof and all were happy to come to know each other and become friends. There was so much respect for every person's culture and traditions. No one was trying to convince anyone that their culture was better. On the contrary, we were finding so much in common among all of us. After all, each culture and each tradition was built upon the sacrifices of the individuals who wanted to improve the way of life for their own people. There is a piece of truth in every religion and in every faith. But if we pick up only one piece without considering putting it together with the rest, we will miss seeing the whole picture.

Thomas Cromwell, was the movement's regional leader for the Middle East. Together with his wife Katherine, they dedicated their lives to serve and support the missionaries and the members in the Arab world, and in Turkey, Iran, Israel, and Greece. I remember how much we enjoyed Thomas visiting us in Lebanon. He was absolutely our beloved leader. He always cared about us, encouraged us, and acknowledged every sacrifice we made. Although he was the publisher of the *Middle East Times newspaper and he was meeting national heads of state, members of parliament, and scholars, every time he came to visit us in Lebanon, he always treated us like his own friends. He laughed with us, sang Arabic songs, and took us out for dinner many times.*

Through him as well as through Adel, I came to understand what it means to be a parental figure to others. I came to realize the reason they called Rev. and Mrs. Moon "True Parents." It was because they embraced all the members, as well as any person they encountered, as their own children. They worked all their lives to unify religions, races, and nations as one family under God and build bridges where people can communicate and connect and build a world of peace that everyone desires.

During the workshop, I had a special experience. I woke up one morning remembering a dream that I had many years before. I was around 17 years old when I dreamed about a Lebanese Saint named Saint Charbel. He asked me in my dream to become a Catholic nun. But at the same time, I saw myself getting married to someone I didn't see. I started worrying that the Saint would become upset but, to my surprise, he was very happy and he gave us his blessing.

Attending the Divine Principle workshop, I remembered the dream and for the first time I understood its meaning. God wanted me to live like a nun until I received the blessing of marriage.

After we concluded the seven-day workshop and we flew back home, I went to my village and stayed there for a few weeks reflecting upon all that I had learned from the workshop. I wrote down in my diary about the principles and the values that I learned about and that touched me during the workshop.

My Reflections

Who is God?

God is the origin of love and heart.

Why did God create us?

God's motive in creating was to realize His ideal of love. That was the purpose of the creation. In the world where God's ideal is realized, human beings and all things are to live in happiness and harmony centered upon God.

What happened to the first man and woman?

Our first ancestors left the realm of God's love and followed the realm of the archangel's love. In the beginning, God had created the angels as servants to help Him in creating the universe. It took God uncountable years to create the world. Then He created human beings as His own sons and daughters. He created them in His image, His representatives to rule the world, including the angels who were supposed to serve human beings. But in order for man and woman to resemble God completely, they needed time to grow and reach their potential as God's children. Like everything in creation, this follows the same pattern of going through three stages in life: formation, growth, and perfection, which means maturity.

All of creation grows automatically, but human beings are exceptional. Their bodies grow naturally but their minds and their intellect grow according to their choices and the information they put in them. God created human beings in His image, which means they need to have their own freedom to choose and take responsibility for their choices. And because God knew that they needed time to grow while they were still immature, God gave them a commandment to follow until they become mature enough to make their own decisions.

What was the original sin?

Originally, the act of love was an act of creation. It is the most precious and sacred act because a human being is creating another human being. Only God is the creator. But He bestowed all that He had on His own son and daughter, trusting that they would continue creating sons and daughters in His image. In order to do that, God needed to give them the time to grow in order to resemble Him. He needed to give them the freedom and the responsibility to choose, because God created everything within His own choice and His own free will. Then God would bless them as mature human beings, ready to take responsibility for creating another human being in their own image. Otherwise, the fruit of their love, which is their child, would suffer from their immaturity and inability to reflect God fully.

Our first ancestors, before becoming parents, needed to connect to God as the center of their lives so they could learn all God's characteristics—His love, His will, and His intellect—so that they could bequeath them to their children and to their descendants. That's very logical. But, instead, Adam and Eve were more interested in themselves and the archangelic world, which was tempting them to do whatever they pleased. The result was that by relating to each other before they reached maturity, and without God's approval and blessing, they inherited the characteristics of the angels, which are servants. That is why their descendants were born fighting each other and having jealousy and resentment toward each other.

How does God work to restore humankind?

God took responsibility to bring human beings back to Him. The history of humanity has been the history of restoration.

God has been a suffering God. His great sorrow has been that He never had a foothold on the family level, national level, or world level.

God has been working endlessly through saints and sages to awaken people's consciousness and their faith in their creator. But throughout history, God's people, who took responsibility on God's behalf to restore people and bring them back to God, were always persecuted and killed, adding a prolongation to the establishment of God's original ideal.

How is God working today?

God created men and women in His image. The first ancestors left God and followed the archangel Lucifer, living their lives centered upon satisfying their own desires for love, power, and knowledge.

Today, a man and a woman stood up and took responsibility as God's son and daughter to restore the family, and to bring all nationalities, races, and religions to work together as God's beloved children. Rev. and Mrs. Moon have been working for decades to let people understand the ideal of God, who wants to live not only within our hearts but in the midst of our families, communities, and nations.

I learned through the Divine Principle that each one of us needs to take responsibility to become a parental figure to their own family and tribe, representing God to them.

Upon these reflections and upon taking the time to pray and meditate in the peaceful surroundings of my beautiful village, the birthplace of my ancestors, in September 1984 I made the decision to join the Unification Church in Lebanon and become a full-time member.

Understanding Adel's Marriage Blessing

In 1982, at Madison Square Garden in New York, Adel received the Marriage Blessing with Pauline, a sister from New Zealand, along with many brothers and sisters coming from all around the world.

The Unification Church is well known for its mass weddings, which created a lot of criticism and negativity. Well, generally people get to know each other in many different ways. Either they meet by coincidence or someone introduces them. In our church, Rev. Moon suggests the partner. If they agree they accept and receive the blessing of marriage. If they disagree, they can wait for another suggestion or make a suggestion themselves.

After attending the Divine Principle workshop, I came to understand more deeply the meaning of the Marriage Blessing that Adel had participated in.

In order to restore God's original ideal of the creation as one global family, Rev. Moon tries to close the gap and unify the world through international marriages. Throughout history the world became divided into many nationalities, many religions, many ethnicities, and many races. If a person marries someone from an enemy country, their children will love and accept both countries.

Throughout history, people were called to do something different than the norm. In Christianity, the priests and the nuns were called to dedicate their lives to Jesus and to not marry. The same held true for the Buddhist monks and the Muslim Sufis. However, this applied to certain people who were pioneers to do certain missions in a certain time. This is also true in the Unification Church. For a certain time, the members were called to have international marriages and close the gap between races, religions, and ethnicities. In God's eyes, there is no yellow, black, or white; they are all created in His image. The main problem in human history was that the relationship between men and women was not centered upon God but upon self-centered desires. If we can fix that, we can fix all the other relationships.

What the Unification Church teaches us is how we can work together, as men and women, to bring solutions to the world's problems. The reason why God's will was not accomplished until now is because men and women decided to build their families without God at the center, so a world of selfishness, conflict, and division was created. Therefore, restoration cannot be done by individuals, but by both men and women together as couples and as families. Every man and every woman should take responsibility and bring unity to the world. It starts from the family and reaches out to the community, the nation, and the world.

My parents, Elias Akiki and Hélené Abou Karam, at their engagement.

My parents and me, with my two brothers, Ibrahim and Fadi.

With my "spiritual father", Adel Jamati.

*On a picnic near Beirut, with Adel playing guitar, Alfred and his Korean
wife and son, the Narihata couple, and Khaled.*

Adel and Pauline Jamati.

My "spiritual daughter", Vera Sawaya.

Fundraising with Vera, selling oil paintings.

FOUR

The Beginning

I joined Adel and the Japanese couple, Akiko and Toyozo Narihatas, in their center in Antelias, Beirut. The place was so organized and peaceful. I started going fundraising door to door with Adel. After some time, I realized the wisdom behind fundraising. First it brings a good amount of money in a short time, and second it helps to meet all kinds of people: poor and rich, kind and rude, highly educated and poorly educated people, mothers, fathers, children, young, and old. Fundraising is an amazing experience which taught me much about myself as well about the people.

After I became a full-time member, I started seeing Rev. Moon and True Parents in my dreams. My first dream about Rev. Moon was seeing him push me hard onto the ground to save me from a gunshot which hit him in his shoulder. Despite getting hurt in my place, he felt so sorry for pushing me down.

On the other hand, since I moved out of my home, my parents played an important role in supporting me and letting me go. When I reflect about that time, I feel so much love and appreciation for my parents. They were truly prepared by heaven. In the Middle East, children, especially daughters, don't leave home and live somewhere else unless they are getting married. My father was an open-minded person and my mother united with me; we were truly one heart and one spirit. She even started seeing Rev. Moon in her dreams and she realized that he was a man of God. Also, both my parents loved Adel and trusted him, and they believed that he would take good care of me like his sister.

Also at that time, my brother, Ibrahim, was working in Saudi Arabia so he was helping my parents financially. In this way I didn't need to worry about them. He even helped me many times when I needed to travel and later when I started having children. Ibrahim was a very generous young man, he used to help many relatives as well. Because of him, I was free to dedicate my life to God and True Parents and join the church, becoming the first sister to join in Lebanon.

Vera Joined

Meantime, Vera started visiting us often and Adel began giving her lectures. She was very inspired by the peaceful atmosphere at the center and more and more she started feeling at home. At the same time, a young man named Khaled contacted Adel and started coming to our center and listening to Divine Principle lectures. He had met a church member when he was visiting England and through him, he found out about us.

In the summer of 1985, together with Vera, Khaled, and Adel, I went to Greece to participate in a 21-day regional workshop. We had the most memorable time, visiting many beautiful and historical places in Greece, like the Acropolis in Athens and the Meteora where the monks built their monasteries on top of the sky-high rocks. We also went to the beach a few times to enjoy the warm Mediterranean Sea.

When we came back to Lebanon, Khaled decided to join us as a full-time member. He started going fundraising sometimes with Adel and sometimes with me. Unfortunately, after a few months, Khaled decided that this kind of life was not what he wanted, so he left the center.

At that time Pauline came to join Adel and start their family. With Pauline joining us, we experienced a whole new beginning. As a strong fundraiser, with a lot of experience when she was in the United States, she suggested to Adel that instead of selling small prints with a small profit, why didn't we try selling oil paintings on canvas. So, Adel ordered a few hundred paintings from America to be shipped to Lebanon. Meanwhile, the Narihata couple left and went back to Japan.

Then, my beloved friend Vera decided to join us as a full-time member in the beginning of 1986. Having Vera join me as a full-time member in Lebanon was the best reward that I received. She was for me more than a friend and more than a sister. She believed in me and she wanted to follow my footsteps. Our love for each other helped us to overcome a lot of challenges as the first sisters who joined in Lebanon. Her love will be forever engraved in my heart.

Fundraising and Witnessing

Fundraising with oil paintings was a big hit. I started going with Vera every day. We carried small, medium, and large paintings. We rolled the canvases up and carried them under our arms and we went selling them door to door. Then we started going up to the mountain and visiting the villages. Fundraising with Vera was a most memorable experience. We enjoyed each other's company. We talked a lot, and we laughed a lot. We sang, we joked, and sometimes we argued, but we always ended up on good terms.

Fundraising in Lebanon was a rich cultural experience of the people and their traditions. The Lebanese are generous people and have an optimistic nature. Despite the unstable situation of the country, they were always hopeful that better days were ahead. So, when we knocked on their doors and showed them our beautiful paintings, they were excited to buy them to decorate their homes. And if they didn't buy, they would offer us a cup of coffee or some fruits and cookies.

Meanwhile, Pauline started teaching English in a community college near the center. This gave her the opportunity to meet young Lebanese people and build good teacher-student relations with them. The Lebanese people in general like to connect with foreigners and are open to hear new ideas and different thoughts and philosophies.

Within a few months, Pauline invited one of her students to come to the center and meet all of us. His name was Adel Habr. He was a very serious and respectful young man, but also he was curious and suspicious about us. After visiting a couple of times and coming to know us, and especially connecting to Adel, Pauline's husband, he started enjoying our friendship and he even started inviting us to meet his parents and siblings. His mother, the same as my mother, was happy to cook for us and to invite us many times for dinner at her house.

As we started expanding and growing, we focused upon doing neighborhood activities, which our movement calls "home church", including reaching out to our mothers. We invited them to our center for a nice gathering once a month. In this way, my mother came to know Vera's mother and Adel Habr's mother, and later Josephine's mother joined us as well.

Upon this foundation of trust, Adel started giving Divine Principle lectures and movement introductions to Pauline's student, Adel Habr.

I continued fundraising together with Vera for almost five years. Sometimes we encountered different challenges and harsh realities because of the situation of the country. Many times, the electricity went off while we were fundraising, so we climbed many stairs and found our way through the dark hallways. Other times we started running, seeking shelter after hearing gunshots and rockets falling nearby. We waited for a few hours until things calmed down, and then rushed back to the center. At that time, there were no cell phones or public phones to call Adel and Pauline, who were waiting and worrying about us.

FIVE

Church Activities in Lebanon

As we were getting good results from fundraising, Adel and Pauline decided to buy a center instead of continuing to rent. So, with Adel's mother helping financially, we moved to a new apartment, which became the first church center in Lebanon. There was other good news: Adel and Pauline welcomed the birth of their first child, Hassan.

Within two years of purchasing the apartment, Adel, with the help of $20,000 from his brother George, bought a unit and made it into an art shop for painting and framing.

Besides fundraising, we decided to focus on witnessing. I told Adel that I would like to experience what it means to be a missionary. I chose a village named Ashqout and I packed and took a public bus, aiming to stay by myself doing fundraising and witnessing. The first day when I went fundraising door to door, I had no results at all. It was very tiring as the houses in the village were far from each other, some up on the hills and others down in the valley.

However, I had an interesting experience. As I was sitting on a rock resting after a few hours of going around, I met a high school kid playing soccer by himself in the field. He approached me, asking if I needed any help. We started chatting and I explained to him about the purpose of my visit. He was deeply moved by my talk about God and our principles and values and he started sharing about his childhood. He told me that when he was around 12 years old a relative of his family abused him and this affected his entire life. Then he left without leaving any way to reconnect. I felt like he just wanted to reveal a secret that had been hidden in his chest for a long time and share it with a stranger who would not judge him. It was a moment of confession and liberation.

As I continued my fundraising, I felt deeply the heart of God whose sorrow is beyond our imagination, as He is carrying all the pain and the hurt that people have done to each other.

Later in the afternoon, I started thinking about finding a motel to spend the night. But instead, I went to a Catholic school nearby where, during my last year in high school, I had stayed with schoolmates for a study retreat. Well, I found out that they did not accept visitors anymore, but, as it had become late, they let me spend one night there. The next day, I started fundraising early hoping to compensate for the day before. It was very hard to sell paintings as most of the houses had already been decorated and had plenty of pictures on their walls.

As I kept going, I entered a small alley which led me to a big house. I noticed some ladies sitting on the balcony sipping coffee. I waved from afar and they waved back to me, which encouraged me to go straight to their house and ring the doorbell. A young woman, my age, welcomed me and invited me to join them for coffee. Her name was Nohad. She introduced me to her mother and her sister, Fadia. All of them looked very friendly and happy to meet me. I started showing them my paintings, but they were more interested to chat and learn more about my background. As the time went by, I realized that I should say goodbye and continue my fundraising.

To my surprise, Nohad was very inspired to meet me and she invited me to come back and have dinner with them and even spend the night in their house. So, for the next two days I continued fundraising in the village and went back to Nohad's house to sleep. I shared with Nohad about our movement and our principles and values and, before leaving for Beirut, I promised to come back to see her again. I couldn't wait to share my experiences with everyone when I arrived at the center. We all started planning to do more outreach activities in preparation for our next summer workshop, this time in Turkey.

Members and Friends

Meanwhile, our regional leader, Thomas Cromwell, came to visit. Every time Thomas visited us, we felt so inspired and rejuvenated. He was like a king checking up on his people; always encouraging us, complementing our work, and making us feel so special. Because of all his hard work and tremendous sacrifices for the Middle East, we could be connected closely to all the international activities and the worldwide movement. As the publisher of the Middle East Times newspaper, Thomas tried to find high profile people in education, economic, political, and religious sectors in the Middle East and invite them to attend international conferences promoting dialogue and constructive communication for the sake of peace in the region.

At the center, while Vera and myself started taking turns in helping Pauline with her baby, we came up with the idea to ask our contacts to join us in fundraising. As we were few in number, we thought it would be nice for our friends and siblings to join us in fundraising and to come with us to attend the summer workshop. The plan was successful, and within a short time we organized ourselves in a group of six and we started going fundraising two by two: Vera with her sister, Sona, and myself with Josephine, my high school friend. We also reached out to Khaled as well as my brother, Fadi.

In this way, everyone was able to earn money to buy their tickets and to travel with us to attend a seven-day workshop, this time in Turkey. It was a memorable experience for me and Vera to be able to share our principles and values with our friends and our siblings. We really felt that God's love had multiplied and all our sacrifices over the last few years had started bringing good results.

I tried to reach out to Nohad, my friend who had welcomed me into her house and let me stay with her for a few days during my fundraising in Ashqout. Unfortunately, she couldn't participate in any activities because her father was very strict about letting her go out anywhere.

Vivian

I had a friend in middle school named Vivian. She lived near me in Beirut on the next street. Although we went to different high schools and colleges, we continued to see each other as neighbors. After I joined the church, I would always try to meet Vivian when I visited my parents.

I invited her a few times to the church center and she listened to Adel's lectures. But because the of the difficult situation in Lebanon, I began to lose touch with her especially so after I left to Cypress, then to Greece, and then to Egypt. But Adel kept connection with her and she attended Divine Principle workshop then decided to apply for the blessing. Unfortunately, her blessing didn't work as the brother was from a Muslim background and he didn't accept it.

Vivian stayed connected to our church and has continued to support our principles and values and to participate in church activities.

SIX

My Turn Has Come

The first day of every year is celebrated as God's Day in our church. We pray at midnight and we offer our gratitude to our Heavenly Father for all the blessings of the past year. We also set new plans and goals for the coming new year.

As we were celebrating the first day of the year 1989, Adel and Pauline asked me to join them in a meeting in the prayer room. They looked very serious and formal, which made me wonder what was happening.

Adel offered a prayer first and then he started talking about the importance of marriage and the responsibility for each one of us to build an ideal family centered upon God. "Blessing" in our church means getting married. As I was listening to Adel and looking at Pauline, who was smiling from ear to ear, my heart started beating fast when I realized that maybe it was my time now to get Blessed.

One important condition we do as we prepare to receive the Blessing is to fast for seven days. Yes, every person who attended the Blessing needed to fast for seven days, no food, only water. It is a condition that the members do voluntarily in order to restore all the mistakes of our ancestors and the suffering that humankind has caused to God and to our fellow human beings throughout history. Luckily, I had done this a while before, becoming a candidate for the Blessing after dedicating many years in the church doing fundraising and witnessing.

As I was preparing to leave the country to go to the Blessing at the beginning of January, fighting started suddenly and Beirut airport was shut down. The situation became dangerous and all of us were worried that I would not be able to leave. As the condition of the country became unstable, Adel suggested taking the boat to Cyprus and from there to fly to Seoul, South Korea. So, there I was with my little suitcase taking an overnight trip by boat to Cyprus and from there flying to Singapore, as there were no direct flights to Korea, and staying two days in a hotel before continuing to Seoul. I arrived on January the seventh and I was picked up from the airport together with many members who were arriving from all around the world.

Our gathering was at the McCol factory. Our church in Korea had built this huge factory to produce a carbonated drink made of barley, using high quality water from a mineral spring. As I registered and found out where to stay, I started hearing the beautiful voices of singing, clapping, and praying coming from the hallway. I joined brothers and sisters, feeling God's presence and God's love and joy surrounding us as we came together from different nationalities, races, and ethnicities as one global family.

The next day, after having breakfast, I attended several lectures and talked to many people, enjoying the beautiful international platform that

True Parents had created for all of us. That evening we learned that the next day Rev. Moon would come and start the matching process, so we needed to sleep early and get up early the next day.

That night, I reflected so deeply about my life in the movement and how God had picked me up like a hair from the dough and guided me all the way to here. Not so many people will understand the process but myself I did. In order to restore the world, we need to sacrifice our romantic love and let a man of God choose a soulmate for us. Then the romance will come after that.

Rev. Moon discovered this after so many years of prayers and sacrifices. He continuously asked God how to bring unity to this world of so many religions, races, and nationalities? The answer was inter-religious and international marriages. In this way, the family unites the divided society and divided community. And the key to the success of these marriages is that each member takes responsibility in loving their spouse, no matter what background they come from, and let God be the center of that relationship. It is a noble task that only prepared people can really understand.

The Blessing

On January 9, we gathered all together in a big hall, brothers on one side and sisters on the other side. True Parents entered, and the whole crowd stood up with one heart and one beat, as if heaven and earth were becoming one. Rev. Moon began with prayer, and then he started strolling around us and talking to the members and choosing their partners.

I truly felt the parental heart of True Father trying to gather his children from different countries who used to be enemy countries in the past, like Korea and Japan, England and Germany, Russia and America, and so forth. God loves all the people the same and He wants their children to live in peace and harmony and build God's kingdom on earth as in heaven. I heard Rev. Moon many times asking "Can you take care of your wife as God's beloved daughter? Can you take care of your husband as God's representative?" He was always emphasizing the importance of bringing God into our relationship and relating to each other as God's beloved children.

"How old are you?" His voice came from behind my shoulder. "I am 28," I replied. He asked me to follow him and, as the father of the bride, he escorted me to my husband to be. I didn't look at the brother's face. We just bowed to True Father as a way to thank him and left the room together, hearing brothers and sisters clapping each time a couple got matched.

"My name is Larry and I am an American," the brother said. I looked at his face for the first time and replied "My name is Marie Thérése and I come from Lebanon." He looked at me with a big smile and said, "Wow, all the way from Lebanon!" Then we went directly to the registration table where we wrote our names and from where we came, and we signed that we agreed with True Father's choice for us. Both of us were determined to accept any person that True Father chose for us.

Many members take time before they agree and, if they don't, they may go back to the room hoping for another choice. The core idea is that no matter who the person was, I would accept him as God's child and build with him a God-centered family. Of course, many challenges may occur if the candidates were very different in the color of their skin, or their ethnicities, or religions. But God had prepared some faithful members who really were willing to accept the challenge and to try to overcome the racial and religious barriers, and even sometimes physical appearance as well. So, it was truly upon each one's decision to accept or to reject. As for me and Larry, we accepted the choice right away. This didn't mean that we thought that everything would be sweet and easy, but we took the first step to make it work.

During this time, I learned that Larry's youngest brother had cancer and was fighting for his life. I also learned that Larry had particpated in the Madison Square Garden Blessing in 1982. He was matched then to a European sister, but she left the church before they started their family life. As I was coming to know more about Larry's life, I realized how much he had needed to endure, and how he waited for almost 15 years in the church until he received the Blessing.

As we were rehearsing for the big day, I got busy trying on white dresses handmade by Korean elder sisters. Then on January 12, 1275 couples stood up so proud and so bright outside the McCol factory, walking step by step toward the big room where True Parents, Rev. and Mrs. Moon, were sprinkling holy water and blessing the brides and the bridegrooms. Then the couples exchanged their rings and shared the holy wine that True Parents offered, and all together with one heart pledged that, no matter what we will face in the future, we will love, sacrifice, and unite with each other in good times and in difficult times. The ceremony was so profound and so meaningful as we stood side by side with people from all around the world, promising our Heavenly Father that we would dedicate ourselves and our families to build a peaceful world centered upon His ideal. We ended with three cheers of *"mansei"*, which means "victory" in Korean.

In the evening of the same day, we enjoyed a beautiful performance prepared by members for this occasion. Then Rev. and Mrs. Moon offered a few Korean songs, and the whole room transformed into a beautiful and heavenly symphony.

The next day it snowed and the whole place was engulfed with a beautiful white blanket. It was like nature was putting on her white dress and receiving the Blessing as well. As the temperature started dropping and the members started packing up and leaving, I said goodbye to Larry and went to another church center where I stayed two more weeks, visiting Korea and enjoying sightseeing and learning about the Korean culture and traditions. Meanwhile, Larry joined the American members who decided to stay in Korea and learn the language as well, helping to promote the newly published newspaper, *Segye Ilbo*.

When Rev. Moon matched and blessed the couples, and they were married in a religious ceremony that we call "The Blessing," the reality was more like an engagement than a wedding. The couples didn't live together as husbands and wives until a few years later, depending on their missions and situations. During that period, they would come to know each other very well by exchanging letters and visiting each other, as well as coming to know each other's parents and family.

SEVEN

Cyprus and Greece

I came back to Lebanon toward the end of January, full of inspiration and excitement, just to face a dangerous and unstable situation in the country. Although there was a ceasefire, we were not able to do fundraising or any church activities, and within a month the situation had deteriorated. The fighting between different militias accelerated and the shelling and the bombardment started reaching close to our center. Facing this dangerous reality, Adel decided that all of us should leave the country until there was a ceasefire.

In March 1989, Adel and Pauline, who was pregnant with her second child, and their son, Hassan, together with Vera and myself, left Beirut and went to Cyprus. Cleanthes and his wife Theophania were a Cypriot blessed couple who lived in Frenaros, a village not far from Famagusta, a town captured by Turkey in its 1974 invasion, and now part of North Cyprus, which was cut off from the south by a border controlled by the United Nations. Cleanthes and Theophania welcomed us into their home, where they owned a farm and grew potatoes and watermelons. Instead of going fundraising, Vera and I started helping on the farm. It was a very beautiful experience as for the first time in our lives, we spent day in and day out in the fields, digging for potatoes and standing in line tossing the watermelons from one person to the other until they reached the truck.

During that time, I remember having an interesting dream. In my dream I was standing in the middle of the field with a big crowd, and we were looking at the sky which was covered with black birds. As time went by, we started seeing the black birds leaving and white birds coming until they filled up the sky. Then two white horses appeared on the horizon and when the people saw them, they started clapping and cheering. It was such a wonderful dream that I will never forget.

A few months passed and there was no sign of improvement in the situation in Lebanon, so our regional leader Thomas Cromwell asked us to move to Greece and stay in his house.

Greece

It was such a generous act of Thomas and Katherine, who at that time had three boys, Tossa, Anmar, and Alexander, to welcome all of us to their house.

Living in Greece was a totally different experience from Cyprus. Vera and I started going to the *Middle East Times newspaper office in Athens where we tried to help with whatever was needed, like folding and packing the newspapers to be delivered, as well as stamping the envelopes for the subscribers, and so forth. We became friends with a lot of the people who worked at the newspaper. Some of them were Greek and many others were church members who came from different countries to work for the Times. Vera and I became well acquainted with the manager of the newspaper,* Dr. Ramez Malouf, who was Lebanese. We were happy to share with him stories about Lebanon, as well as following up with what was going on in our country and enjoying each other's company.

Already summer had come and there was a plan for Vera and I to attend a Divine Principle workshop in Turkey. But, because the situation in Lebanon had improved and Pauline was getting close to her due date, Adel decided to go back to Lebanon and he asked Vera if she could come back with them to be a helper again for Pauline. I felt sorry for Vera as we really were looking forward to going to Turkey together but, as always, Vera was more than happy to be a helper and a support for Adel and Pauline.

I stayed in Greece for another month, and then I went with a few members by car attend the workshop in Turkey. It was a memorable trip to drive from Athens to Istanbul and enjoy sightseeing in both Mediterranean countries. Katherine, Thomas' wife, came along with us, and when we arrived in the early morning in Istanbul, we went to the airport to pick up Thomas. As we had arrived earlier than we expected, and as we were all exhausted from being awake all night, we parked the van near to the airport and we fell asleep. Within a few hours, we woke up hearing so many noises and found ourselves surrounded by so many people. It turned out that we had parked at a bus station! It was such a funny experience that we shared it with Thomas after we picked him up.

The seven-day workshop in Istanbul was mostly attended by a big group of young people who came all the way from Iran. In fact, one of the Iranian members who came at that time was Ahmad Azhari who was

Blessed later in 1992 to Vera. Also, Adel Habr came from Lebanon to attend the workshop. As always, we all had wonderful experiences listening to Divine Principle lectures and visiting historical places like Aya Sophia, the National Museum, and Ankara, the capital of Turkey.

After we said goodbye and went back to Greece, a letter from Larry was waiting for me at the office of the *Middle East Times. He had written to tell me that he had left Korea and gone back to the States because his brother Paul, who was fighting cancer, had passed away. I felt so sorry that I never was able to meet Paul. He was* almost exactly my age, 28 years old.

As I stayed at Thomas' house, I enjoyed spending time with his children and when I celebrated my birthday with them on August 31, I got the news that Pauline had given birth to a baby girl on my birthday. That was a nice surprise.

A New Mission

One morning in September, Thomas invited me to share a cup of coffee with him before he left for the office. He started talking about the *Middle East Times* office in Egypt and how important it was to keep that branch going. Then he continued talking about the purpose of having a publication which promotes freedom of speech and which encourages dialogue between different religions and cultures in the region.

Suddenly he looked at me and said, "Would you like to manage our office in Cairo?" That was a big surprise for me. I didn't know what to say. So, Thomas asked me to take my time and think about it, and he added, "The American brother who used to take care of the Cairo office has already gone back to the States and I don't have any representative there, only a few Egyptian employees. I thought you would be the best choice as you know the Arabic language and you studied journalism."

After Thomas left, I went back to my room and tried to reflect deeply about his suggestion. I stayed inside all day, thinking and praying. I had always wanted to have a mission, but to go all by myself to Egypt, a Muslim country, with no members or Blessed families there, I thought that was a big task.

A few days passed and I was still hesitant to give an answer to Thomas. One evening as I was watching the sunset from the balcony, I started thinking about the missionaries who were sent overseas to witness and represent True Parents in their mission country. I thought mostly about the French missionary, Mr. Remi Blanchard, who came to Lebanon and found Adel and Adel found me. If not for him, I would not be here today. That night, I made up my mind. Somehow, although I had studied journalism and, since my childhood, I had been telling everyone that my dream was to become a journalist, going to Egypt was more like a mission to take and a responsibility to fulfill rather than a personal goal to achieve.

The next day, I told Thomas that I would be happy to go to Cairo and work for the Middle East Times office there. Then I sent a message to Adel and Pauline informing them about my new mission. Also, I wrote a letter to Larry telling him about my latest assignment. Within a week, I said goodbye to Greece and headed to Egypt. A new chapter began in my life, as a pioneer sister in the land of the Pyramids.

⁂

EIGHT

Egypt

The land of the Pyramids and the "gift of the Nile" is how Egypt is described in the history books. It never occurred to me that I would go and live there for many years.

It was early evening time when I arrived in Cairo in the middle of September 1989. Thomas had already arranged with one Egyptian employee, named Hisham, to pick me up from the airport. I was surprised by Hisham renting a limousine to take me to the apartment where the American brother used to live. I guess he was trying to show off!

From the first moment I stepped in Cairo, I felt a heavy heart. Looking from the car window, I saw children with bare feet and women with long dresses and head coverings. Watching the men pushing their fruit and vegetable carts in the middle of the streets and buses overflowing with people honking to clear the way, my heart started beating fast. I felt lonely, not knowing what kind of future lay ahead.

Next day I woke up early in the morning hearing the voice of the

Imam calling for prayers at 5 a.m.: *"Allahu akbar, allahu akbar,"* which means God is great. Although it was familiar to me to hear the Muslim prayers, as in Lebanon half of the population were Muslims, I used to hear it from afar as I lived in a Christian neighborhood. I also realized that there was a mosque on every corner of the city, and sometimes, if the mosque was too small, men would be sitting on the sidewalks, listening to the imam's sermon and performing their bowing while reciting verses from the Quran.

The next day, as I headed to the Middle East Times office, which was around 10 minutes' walk from the apartment, I was happily surprised by the neighborhood which looked really nice. The district of Zamalek is a cosmopolitan neighborhood in Cairo where a lot of European expatriates live. It has villas, surrounded by gardens and trees, as well as international restaurants and art museums. It was a nice relief for me to find out that our office and the building where I was to live were located in such a lovely area.

The newspaper office was a small humble place with a few desks and chairs, but what was interesting was that there were two employees, one in the morning and one in the afternoon, whose job it was to answer the doorbell and make coffee for guests.

Beside Hisham, who was the marketing manager, there were two free-lancers, one Egyptian and one American, who provided articles about local events. Also, there was an American professor named Dr. John Munro, who taught at the American University in Cairo and who wrote a weekly column for the *Middle East Times.* The bureau manager of the office was Mr. Ahmad Lotfy. His main responsibility was to deal with the

Egyptian authorities regarding any legal issues for the newspaper and the employees.

After spending two months all by myself in Cairo, I met an American brother named Walter Gottesman. He had been sent to Egypt as a missionary a few years before, but when I arrived in Egypt he was traveling to the States with his wife and daughter. He returned to Cairo by himself to stay for some time.

The *Middle East Times*

As I started getting acquainted with the people and the place, I realized within a few months that most of the people who worked at the newspaper were taking advantage by doing little and getting paid a lot. So, the first thing I did was to get rid of one of the workers making tea and coffee. I kept the other, not to make coffee but to do errands for the office.

Also, I heard from the writers that their articles had been published a few months ago but they hadn't been paid yet. I contacted our office in Athens and I made sure to pay the freelancers right away. The biggest issue was Hisham, who would come to the office for an hour or two, make a few phone calls, drink his coffee, and then leave. He rarely brought any advertisements or subscriptions. He was good at talking and socializing with everyone in the office as well, making sure that whatever I needed, he was there to help. But as a marketing manager, he was bringing maybe just one ad a month for the newspaper, and sometimes none. I knew from the beginning that he was not the right person for the job but I didn't want to take dramatic action by firing many people at once. Instead, I rolled up my sleeves and went to work myself.

As I wrapped up the year 1989 and started a new year in Egypt, I looked for a secretary who could help me in organizing the office, answering phone calls, and following up with the freelancers. Then I got a list of the foreign companies and the addresses of the expatriates who lived in Cairo and started sending the newspaper to them and inviting them to subscribe. I also tried to reach out to the Egyptian companies who were interested in letting the foreigners who lived in Egypt know about their products or their services and asked them to put advertisements in our newspaper.

Within a few months, we began to see more ads in the newspaper, as well as more subscriptions. I remember one day receiving a phone call from our editor Ramez Malouf in Greece, congratulating me on getting one full page advertisement and telling me how excited he was to see our Egyptian office catching up.

Two new journalists joined our newspaper: George Shadroui, who was an American Lebanese, and Giles Trendle, who came from England. Our office became more and more upbeat and professional people came to work for us. Then it was time to say goodbye to Hisham, as Thomas hired a new Egyptian marketing manager.

Welcoming Adel's Family and Church Members

By mid-1990 I received a phone call from Adel telling me that the situation in Lebanon was getting worse once again and they were not able to do fundraising, and his store was not having any customers, so he was thinking of moving to Egypt. He came first and then Pauline and the children followed him later. Vera moved to Cyprus and stayed with the

Cypriot couple for a while. Then she went to France and joined the fund-raising team to raise money for Lebanon.

Meanwhile, three brothers came from the United States to spend 40 days in Egypt and do outreach missions. Thomas connected them to a Sufi group who lived in Alexandria. Together with Adel, we went with them to Alexandria and spent a few days with this group, learning about Sufism, their mysticism, and their practices, and building a bridge to connect them to our principles and values. Later that year, we learned that the whole Sufi group with their leader went to New York to attend a 40-day International Leadership Seminar, a program set up to introduce Muslim leaders to Unificationism.

As Adel started working at the *Middle East Times* office, Thomas asked him to work on the legal issues which emerged as the newspaper started having a regular income from advertising and subscriptions. Ahmad Lotfy left our newspaper, so we hired an Egyptian lawyer to give us advice.

We also welcomed Erwin Franzen, who had been with the Middle East Times from its beginnings in Cyprus, and later moved with the paper to Greece, where he was joined by his Japanese wife. He was originally from Luxembourg but was fluent in English and had worked on the New York City Tribune. He became the editor of the newspaper. They had one son at that time.

Within a few months, we heard that the situation in Lebanon had deteriorated dramatically, so I called my parents to check up on them. They told me that my brother Ibrahim, who was working in Saudi Arabia at that time, had encouraged them to leave the country and go to Cyprus, the closest country to Lebanon, until the situation calmed down. They were hesitating as they had never traveled before, and besides they didn't know anyone in Cyprus and they didn't speak the language. Although they were going to travel with my youngest brother, Fadi, still they weren't sure about it. I suggested to them to come to Egypt instead and stay with me. They liked that idea better and they felt more secure to come to a place where their daughter lived and where the people spoke the same language.

Welcoming my Parents and Larry

To welcome my parents in Egypt, I rented a nice apartment close to a grocery store and a public garden so it would be easy for my parents to function. For the first time after I left home in 1984 to join the church in Lebanon, I had the opportunity to live with my parents again for almost four months. During that time, I shared with them about True Parents and tried on a daily basis to lecture the Divine Principle to them in a simple way so they could understand it. My mom in particular was deeply touched by our values and our teaching, and we started praying together every day. She even started seeing True Father in her dreams.

I wrote to Larry about all that was happening in Egypt with new people working at the *Middle East Times,* Adel moving to Egypt with his family, and my parents escaping the war in Lebanon and staying with me in Cairo. He decided to come and visit me at that time so he could meet my parents, as well as come to know Adel and Pauline and visit the newspaper office.

Summer 1990 was a memorable summer as I welcomed Larry to Egypt and introduced him to my parents, who fell in love with him. Every evening we had a nice dinner with my parents and played card games. My father was able to communicate with Larry with his simple English, but not my mom. Still, she could convey what she wanted to say by her warm smile and generously serving us with her delicious homemade food.

I introduced Larry to all the Middle East Times employees, and we talked a couple of times about the possibility that he could move to Egypt and join me in working for the newspaper. Although Larry was hoping that I would come to live with him in Korea, he realized that it was much needed to have members staying in Egypt and working for the *Middle East Times. We spent some time with Adel and Pauline,* and one day we had an outing with the Franzens to Alexandria and enjoyed a picnic on the beach.

Ten days had passed quickly, and it was time to say goodbye to my sweetheart and go back to the normal daily routine at the office.

My parents returned to Lebanon after spending four months in Egypt, as the situation in Lebanon had improved. In September 1990, I celebrated my first year being in Egypt.

Challenges

As I continued working at the *Middle East Times office during the second year, I faced once again many challenges to overcome. First, I found out that the* employee who I had kept was stealing money from the office, so I fired him. Then I realized that the new Egyptian marketing manager, whose salary was very high, wasn't able to bring results, so I took the decision to ask him to leave.

On the other hand, our editor George Shadroui left the office and went back to the States after working with us for a year, so Thomas asked our church member Erwin Franzen to take his position. He also hired a new marketing manager, a Scottish retiree who lived in Cairo and who had good connections with expatriates. I also hired a few more Egyptians for different kinds of jobs as freelancers and in marketing. I welcomed as well a new English writer to replace Giles Trendle, who had left the newspaper.

Our office became busier, and we started having more revenue as the newspaper had more people working and promoting it. This alerted the Egyptian authorities, so they came knocking on our door. Most of the time in the second year we tried, Adel and myself, to negotiate with the Egyptian attorney about how to avoid paying taxes because our newspaper was published in Athens, not in Egypt, and we were already paying the taxes in Greece.

Meanwhile, far from the hectic work at the office, I started making good friendships. Ashraf, the new financial manager, introduced me to his wife, Audette, and we became good friends. Also, I became a good friend of a new freelancer named Linda, who was half Lebanese and half American, and her husband, Assef El Bayat, an Iranian professor who taught at the American University in Cairo. During one of Thomas' visits, he introduced me to Gihan, a professor of English at Ain Shams University, and we became good friends.

My matching with Lawrence David Bond (Larry),
January 9, 1989, in South Korea.

Receiving the blessing of marriage, January 12, 1989.

*Larry's parents, Donald and Beverly Bond,
and his siblings, Paul and Debbie.*

Larry's grandparents, Elmer and Rachel (Marie) Bond.

NINE

Starting our Family

In spring 1991, Larry left Korea after spending two years there and joined me in Egypt to start our family. Linda and Assef offered us their lovely house in Garden City while they were visiting the States for two months. During that time, a Korean brother came to visit Egypt, so we welcomed him to stay with us for two weeks. Before he left, he asked us to choose a nice hotel to go to for the weekend and he would pay for it as a gift of gratitude for welcoming him to our place. Larry suggested going to El Fayoum city, located around 62 miles southwest of Cairo, and staying at Helnan Auberge Fayoum, a hotel where Sir Winston Churchill had stayed when he visited Egypt during World War II. That was a nice gift for our honeymoon.

Larry joined me at the *Middle East Times*, working as copy editor and features writer, and we rented a small apartment ten minutes from the office. It was a special time for us as we worked together in the same office, sharing the same schedule, and interacting with the same people, as well as making good friends. We enjoyed having lunch together at the nice restaurant located in the Marriott hotel in Zamalek, where we lived, or going to the Meridien hotel for a nice dinner at the Nile River. Many times we were invited by our Egyptian friends for homemade Egyptian food when we came to meet their families.

Our First Child

In the middle of August 1991, as the temperature in Cairo rose very high and the desert climate became very dry and dusty, I suddenly started feeling weak and sick so I scheduled an appointment to see a doctor. To my surprise, I found out that I was pregnant. We were happy but also unprepared as we didn't expect it that soon! Both our parents were very excited to hear the news as it was their first grandchild.

Meanwhile, Adel and his family went back to Lebanon and Erwin's family had left Egypt for Cyprus in 1990. Once again, I found myself all alone, except this time I had my husband standing by my side, building a foundation in Egypt. Also, we had our elder brother Walter Gottesman visit us from time to time and check up on us.

One time, as I was going for a routine checkup, my doctor told me that in my regular blood test they found out that I had toxoplasmosis. This is an infection caused by a parasite which comes mostly from undercooked meat, unwashed fruits and vegetables, or contaminated utensils. Because we were eating at restaurants often, that was probably the case. This news made us so worried, and we started researching to know more about this condition. Most of the information that we found through the medical books and internet indicated that this parasite would affect the baby. Somehow my doctor didn't have a clear answer about how serious this could be!

We decided to check with other doctors and ask their opinion. Most of the doctors told us that normally the toxoplasmosis would cause the baby to be born abnormal and they suggested abortion. That was shocking news. For the first time we felt so alone and everything around us was so dark and heavy. I even started having difficult experiences in my daily life, like when I took a taxi, the driver would be talking about sick children. When I turned on the TV, the program would be about abnormal babies. I felt like a spiritual attack on our firstborn baby.

The only one who really didn't accept the doctor's recommendation was Larry. He suggested going to the States and checking with the doctors there. I was not in the mood to travel for over fifteen hours to California and to visit Larry's parents, whom I had never met before, in this kind of situation! But I really wanted to unite with my husband as my only hope to save my baby, so we notified the newspaper's office and left for California.

Larry's parents were so happy to see us. They made everything possible to make me feel at ease and at home. They arranged the doctor's appointment and paid for all the expenses. When we visited the doctor, he referred us to a lab which specialized in toxoplasmosis so we went there and they took a sample of my blood to analyze it. Within a few days the results came back. They said that although I had toxoplasmosis in my blood, it didn't hurt the baby. They found out the history of this parasite in my blood, that I had had it before I was pregnant, so that the baby was immune to it. Otherwise, if I had gotten it during my pregnancy, it would have gone directly to the baby and affected him.

That was the best news I had heard in a long time. Our unity as a blessed couple saved our firstborn.

Following this good news, we went and visited Larry's paternal grandparents, Elmer and Rachel Bond. I was so delighted to meet them, especially because I had never met my grandfathers, who had passed away before I was born. I knew both my grandmothers, who died when I was a teenager. Larry told me that his favorite childhood memories were when he used to visit his grandparents' place. They were such warm and sweet elder couples. They were so happy to see us, and we felt at home.

After spending two weeks in California, we returned to Egypt with our healthy baby growing peacefully in my tummy. I continued working at the *Middle East Times during my pregnancy, despite it becoming harder to climb the stairs to the third floor every time I went to the office.*

Donald Elias Bond was born on April 25th, 1992, three weeks earlier than his due date. Thank God, he was fully grown and healthy, with a head full of hair. We decided to give him the name of both grandfathers because he was the first grandchild to both. Within a month after Donald was born, my mother came to help me and spent a few months with us.

Donald was a very happy and sociable boy. Every time I took him out in his stroller, he would be smiling and waving to everyone. I remember once when I was walking with him on the street with a bag of chips in his hands—he was around two years old at that time—he started giving chips to everybody passing by. That was his personality since his childhood; a friendly and generous person.

Welcoming a New Church Leader to Egypt

Within a few months after Donald was born, we welcomed Young Jin Kim as the new church leader in Egypt, together with his wife Shin Sook Kwak, the eldest daughter of Rev. Kwak, and their two children. During that time, I felt that a new providence had started in Egypt, with more focus upon spiritual activities and outreach to our Muslim community. The Kim family rented a place near our apartment, and we started attending Sunday service in their house. My life in Egypt started looking more like my life in Lebanon—a small group of brothers and sisters trying to build a spiritual foundation in the country.

At that time, I had an interesting dream about True Parents' first and second sons, Hyo Jin and Heung Jin. Although Hyo Jin was alive at that time, I saw him meeting his brother Heung Jin, who had died in a car accident a few years earlier. I can't describe how beautiful and joyful that occasion was. Heung Jin was wearing a traditional Korean outfit with a crown on his head and Hyo Jin was wearing simple jeans and a T-shirt. The two brothers embraced profoundly, and the atmosphere was overflowing with love and gratitude.

Welcoming Larry's Family

As Donald turned four months old, we welcomed Larry's parents and sister for the first time in Egypt. They were so excited to see Donald, their first grandchild, and they decided to take all of us on a Nile cruise and visit the famous tourist attractions in Luxor and Aswan. Although we had lived in Egypt for many years, we just knew the Pyramids and the national museum. So when my in-laws came to visit, we enjoyed having a vacation and getting to know the famous places in Egypt.

However, what interrupted this nice trip was realizing what it meant to be a tourist in Egypt. An item which could be worth 10 dollars may jump to the price of 30 dollars or more when the Egyptian salesman finds out that their customers are American or European. That bothered me a lot during my in-laws' visit. I used to argue with the salesmen who were cheating and tripling their prices. Although I had lived in Egypt for many years, and I was aware of the poverty and the illiteracy of the people, it was only when I went on a vacation with Larry's family that I discovered the enormous difference between the minority elite and the poor majority in Egypt.

Vera's Blessing

In 1992, three years after my Blessing, it was Vera's turn. She also traveled to Korea to participate. But at that time, there were a lot of candidates who couldn't travel for different reasons, so they sent their pictures and their portfolios seeking to be matched by True Father. One of them was Ahmad, the brother from Iran, who True Father chose for Vera.

Vera accepted True Father's choice, although she knew she would be facing a lot of challenges when she came back home. She was determined that, by having faith, she would move any mountain.

Everyone was delighted and cheerful when they found out that I was blessed with an American brother. That wasn't the case for Vera.

Besides, it wasn't only that Ahmad was a Muslim brother, but at that time Iran and Lebanon didn't have diplomatic relations so it was hard for Vera and Ahmad to meet or even visit. After Korea, Vera returned to Lebanon to stay with Adel and Pauline until she figured out a way to join Ahmad. Pauline encouraged her to do fundraising and save money for her future family. But it was hard to continue fundraising in Lebanon because the economy was failing, so Adel and Pauline suggested to her to go to France and join the fundraising team there. And this was what she did. It was interesting that Vera could go to France and join our French members at that time. It was something I had wanted to do myself, but I didn't have the chance.

Our Second Child

Donald was growing very well, and Larry and I took turns in taking care of him. Both of us kept working at the *Middle East Times* part time. I went in the morning and Larry went in the afternoon and stayed late to finish his work. Beside working as a copy editor, Larry started writing a weekly column in the newspaper with the title "Cairo Beat." It was inspiring to read Larry's stories, and I enjoyed sending them to his parents in the States.

Five months had passed when I found myself pregnant again. This time it was a very peaceful pregnancy that went very smoothly and without any difficulties. On June 12,1993 Anne Marie was born. It took almost ten hours labor with my first child; with Anne it took only two hours. Again, we wanted to embrace our parents and grandparents and show them our love and appreciation. We gave our daughter the middle name of Larry's mother and grandmother.

Anne was the sweetest and the calmest little child that anyone can wish for. From a young age, Anne was a serious and sincere girl. At that time Donald was very active while Anne was always observing and playing quietly, which made it easier to handle two toddlers at the same time.

By that time, I had stopped working at the *Middle East Times. Larry continued for another year,* and then gave up his desk duties to work at the American University in Cairo as an assistant to Dr. John Munro, who was a columnist at our newspaper. By then, the newspaper was standing on its own feet with many professional employees working at the office, so we left it in good hands after I had worked there for four years and Larry for three.

True Mother's Visit to Egypt

By the end of summer 1993, we received an email from Thomas Cromwell telling us about True Mother's visit to the Middle East. She would be visiting Greece, Turkey, Israel, and Egypt, so we needed to prepare an audience to attend her and to welcome her. It was a big task as we weren't doing any spiritual outreach. Our presence was just to work for the *Middle East Times* and provide an honest voice promoting peace and dialogue and encouraging democracy and openness to the West. Besides, Egypt is a traditional Muslim country which doesn't allow witnessing and spiritual activities. Also, at that time I had two toddlers and Larry was working full time at the American University.

The only thought that came to my mind at that time was the Egyptian charities, as most of them were led by Egyptian women. So, we rolled up our sleeves and started approaching women's clubs and women's groups. On the other side, Thomas started contacting scholars and public figures who in the past had attended our international conferences. Through those connections, he was able to reach out to a high level of Egyptian personalities and to invite them to the event. Meanwhile, a few members from the region and abroad came to help us with the preparation. Our Sudanese brother, Taj Hamad, came from the States to reach out to our Muslim community, and together with Thomas worked very hard to connect and invite university professors and religious figures to attend True Mother's event.

I was very happy to welcome Vera who, after fundraising in France, was able to come to Egypt to support me and to support the event. And for the first time I met Walter's wife, Maureen, and their daughter as they also traveled all the way from the States for this occasion.

Then we welcomed Mrs. Sugiyama, the president of Women's Federation for World Peace, who came together with a few Japanese sisters from Japan to prepare the way for True Mother. We held a few gatherings with some Egyptian women leaders, who promised to invite their members. That was one of the keys which opened the door to bring a lot of people to attend the event. All these women were so inspired to learn about the Women's Federation principles and family values that Mrs. Sugiyama had introduced to them, and they got inspired to apply them in their own organizations.

It was amazing to me to realize how much True Parents invested in different organizations in order to reach out to all nations, religions, and races. The Women's Federation for World Peace was definitely a good channel to reach out to Egyptian communities. Islam is a very strict and traditional religion, and it is very hard to break through. But with Mrs.

Sugiyama introducing our family values, she succeeded in winning the women's hearts, and they promised her to attend the event and bring their members.

By the end of November, we welcomed True Mother in Egypt, and on December 1st she delivered her message in a very nice hotel with around 1,000 attendees. However, unfortunately, as Mother's speech was all about the course of Jesus, and because all the audience were from a Muslim background, many people started leaving in the middle of her talk. Many of them were surprised to hear a spiritual message. Nevertheless, the event went smoothly, and I was asked to offer True Mother a bouquet of flowers at the end of her speech. I remember borrowing Vera's flat shoes to get up to the stage as my feet were swollen from all the preparation needed to be done for the event.

In the evening, we celebrated with True Mother with a nice cake and songs offered by our Sudanese brothers. Next day we said goodbye, wishing True Mother safe travels in the Middle East.

Welcoming the Japanese Sisters

In the beginning of 1994, a new providence started in Egypt with the coming of Japanese sisters as pioneers to represent the Women's Federation for World Peace. Suddenly we welcomed around 30 Japanese sisters to Cairo. They were in three groups of ten. Each group was designated for a different country: one group for Egypt, one for Yemen, and one for Jordan. In the beginning, they all landed in Egypt, and then, within a few weeks, each group left for their mission country.

After being one of the only Blessed couples in Egypt, we were thrilled to be surrounded by our lovely Japanese sisters, who cooked for us and served us a lot of delicious Japanese food. They rented an apartment in our neighborhood, like our Korean couple, and we started gathering together every day for prayers and reflections. The sisters needed a lot of help because of the language barrier. I stepped up to help.

In the beginning, it was just to take them to the embassies to apply for visas so they could travel to their mission countries. Then, with the sisters who stayed in Egypt, I tried to help them in contacting charity organizations where they could volunteer, and also some schools where the sisters offered art classes, teaching origami. Larry volunteered to take the sisters during the weekends for sightseeing to see the Pyramids and the Cairo Museum and show them around. Bit by bit, the sisters representing WFWP started getting involved in volunteering at nursing homes, serving the elderly, and teaching Japanese art at the elementary schools.

Our Third Child

In the midst of all these activities, I became pregnant with my third child. Donald was two years old and Anne was one year old. In my second month of pregnancy, I started bleeding badly. Larry took me to the emergency room where they kept me for one night. The doctor advised me to stay in bed for 15 days, lying on my back in order not to lose the baby. With two toddlers around, it was impossible to do that unless we got some help. We decided to hire an Egyptian housekeeper to help with the house chores and run after the children. The pregnancy was saved and on September 10, 1994, Paul Herbert was born. We gave him the name of Larry's late brother Paul and his grandfather Herbert.

Paul was a very strong boy from the first day he was born. He ate well and slept well. He was the most adventurous among his siblings. Although his character was quiet and observant like Anne, he was more into trying all kinds of jumping and climbing everywhere. Although he might have bumped his head and hurt himself many times, he rarely cried or complained. He had a strong will and endurance.

After Paul was born, we let the housekeeper go, as we couldn't afford to pay for her, and I dedicated my time fully to raising my children.

At the Sphinx and the Great Pyramids, Egypt, summer 1992.

Larry and me, at work at the Middle East Times office in Cairo.

*The Middle East Times Egypt office staff, together with
the visiting publisher Thomas Cromwell and the visiting editor-in-chief,
Dr. Ramez Maalouf.*

My three eldest children, all born in Egypt: Donald, Anne, and Paul.

Introducing the Women's Federation for World Peace to Egyptian women leaders, 1995.

Four generations of Bonds: Larry with his grandfather Elmer, his father Donald, and our eldest son Donald.

My parents, receiving the Blessing in Lebanon, 1995.

*Scott, our fourth child, enjoys the love of his grandmother
in Lebanon in 1997.*

With my husband, my parents, and my three children: three generations.

*My friend Nohad Daghfal attended the blessing in Lebanon in 1997
with her husband and three of her siblings.*

My eldest son Donald with his Uncle Fadi in Lebanon, 1994.

TEN

Our Last Chapter in Egypt

As a stay-at-home mom, I started being more aware than before about my surroundings, and also feeling more sensitive. One example was dealing with the concierge in our building. Generally, in nice residential areas in Cairo, like Zamalek, Mohandessin, and Garden City, every building or house has a concierge who cleans the stairs, picks up the garbage, and so forth. Although it could be handy to have him, many times I got irritated and felt like I was being watched all the time. He was always there, day and night, seeing what we brought home, who was visiting us, what the children were getting, and so on. Before having kids, I didn't pay so much attention, but now being at home all day with my children, I was annoyed by him following our every step.

Another example was whenever I took a taxi to the park, which normally didn't cost more than one dollar. As soon as the driver noticed that we were foreigners, he would charge us double. These types of daily experiences, while raising my children in Egypt, drained me and made me tired.

As time went by and the children grew older, I came to know other mothers who had kids of the same age as mine; some of them Egyptian and others foreigners. We started scheduling play dates for our children and invited friends over to our house. In this way, time went by and these little details faded away.

Giving the Blessing

After leaving the *Middle East Times* office and focusing on my family, I got involved with the Japanese sisters in promoting and introducing Women's Federation for World Peace to the Egyptian community. The sisters started inviting a few Egyptian women they had met at the schools, or at the nursing homes, and cooked Japanese food for them. As I knew Arabic, I helped in translating and explaining the principles and the values of the Federation.

Two of these women continued coming often, and step by step Young Jin Kim started giving them lectures and explaining about the importance of the Blessing and building a family centered upon God. Within a year, they became candidates for the Blessing and they applied for the matching. They were introduced to Muslim candidates from neighboring countries who had sent their photos and portfolio to headquarters. In August 1995, the two Egyptian women received the Blessing, officiated by Young Jin Kim and his wife representing True Parents in Egypt. For the first time in Egypt, we could officiate the Blessing and bring a victorious result.

At the same time in Lebanon, August 1995, my parents renewed their vows and participated in the Blessing, officiated by Adel and Pauline. I remember calling Adel and telling him that I wanted my parents to receive the Blessing. Adel invited my parents and two other older couples, and by satellite, they shared the Blessing with thousands of people throughout the world.

What is interesting is that a new era had started where central figures or Blessed couples could officiate the Blessing in their country, representing True Parents. The foundation was already established and now each one of us can follow the same path of educating, unifying, and Blessing people everywhere. True Parents have established throughout their life a heavenly pattern which each one of us can apply in our daily life.

Leaving Egypt

Proclaiming victory in Egypt didn't last long. As we celebrated God's Day 1996, the first day of the year, together with all our Japanese sisters and the Kim family, little did we know that it would be our last celebration in Egypt. Within a few weeks the Kim family was interrogated by the Egyptian authorities, asking them about the purpose of their stay in Egypt, especially as Young Jin Kim didn't have any job or work permit to show. They also questioned their religious activities, and they were asked to leave the country.

The following week, I received a phone call one morning from the *Middle East Times* office wanting to see me urgently. When I arrived at the office, they showed me an article written in one of the Egyptian newspapers demanding that the Middle East Times pay taxes, and to arrest me since I had managed the newspaper for many years, responsible for filing taxes. I realized that it had something to do with the people who were fired in the past as well as a whole campaign that the Egyptian authorities had launched to kick us out of the country after True Mother's visit.

I contacted Thomas in Greece asking him for advice. He agreed that after True Mother's visit our newspaper had been watched closely by the police. Because Egypt has a lot of foreigners and expatriates working in the country, the authorities waited for the right opportunity and for a good excuse to kick us out.

After a few days of negotiations between our office in Egypt and our office in Greece, Thomas called me at home and asked me to consider leaving the country with my family. I was very surprised by this request, and I explained to Thomas that I really wanted to stay and face the challenges even if it meant for me to go to jail. But Thomas insisted that, as a mother of three kids, I should consider not putting them in danger. He also was worried that they would use me as a hook to hurt our newspaper. So, in order for Thomas to be free to negotiate with the Egyptian authorities, I needed to leave.

In March 1996, Larry and I left Egypt with our three kids and went to Lebanon. This time we were the refugees escaping Egypt and seeking a place to stay. Both my parents and Adel and Pauline welcomed us into their homes. Because it was a sudden move, Larry needed to go back to Egypt and finish his work at the American University. He decided to take Donald with him to ease my load by having only Anne and Paul to take care of. They stayed in Cairo for two months as Larry wrapped up his work at the university and Donald attended a nearby preschool. When they came back, we looked for a place to rent and a new chapter of our lives began in Lebanon.

ELEVEN

Lebanon

When we moved to Lebanon, we knew from the beginning that our final place would be in the United States, but we wanted to give my parents some time to enjoy the grandkids. During our five years together in Egypt, we had visited California and Lebanon a few times so our parents could see the kids.

We felt it was important to encourage a bond between the grandparents and the grandchildren.

The first thing we did when Larry and Donald came back from Egypt was to find a place to rent. We found a furnished apartment in Elissar, in the hills of the Metn area. Then Larry started looking for a job and for a car. In Cairo, it was much easier not to have a car because of the traffic and the difficulties in finding a parking spot in an overpopulated city. Besides, the public transportation was very cheap. But in Lebanon it was different, especially after Larry found a job at an English newspaper called *Eco News,* and he needed to have his own vehicle to go back and forth to the city.

As Donald turned four years old, he started going to kindergarten. In Lebanon the preschool age is three and kindergarten is four. Although we sent him to an English school, half of the subjects were in Arabic language. It was hard on Donald to focus during those classes and he started goofing around from being bored. Although I tried to talk in Arabic with my children, somehow it was hard because Larry spoke only English so most of our conversation at home was in English.

As we settled down in Lebanon, I started reaching out to my cousins that I grew up with as well as to my old friends and contacts. I even went up to Ashqout to visit Nohad and her family. I found out that she and her sibling were already married and had children. Her father had passed away, and one of her siblings, who was working in an Arab country, was married to a Polish girl and they lived nearby. I invited all of them to my house and started having a close relationship with all of them. Then one day, when we had a church event in downtown Beirut, I invited Nohad and her siblings to attend. She came with her husband and brought three of her siblings with their spouses and participated in a holy wine ceremony, pledging to honor their spouses and to have God as the center of their families. That was truly one of my favorite experiences after I came back to Lebanon.

Another wonderful memory I had during my stay in Lebanon was getting to know my neighbor Leila. She lived above us on the third floor with her two daughters. Her place was like an oasis for me; such a peaceful and lovely atmosphere. Her daughters played piano and did artwork. I enjoyed our friendship so much and we have kept connected since then. It was a nice coincidence to know that they had lived in the States before and all had American citizenship as well.

As we started settling down, we received visitors from the States. Larry's newly married sister Debbie and her husband Ted, who were cruising the Mediterranean Sea, came and visited us for two days. They flew to Lebanon when the cruise stopped in Egypt for a few days. They were happy to see the kids and mostly Paul for the first time. We took them to visit Byblos, which is located on the coast of the Mediterranean Sea, 20 miles north of Beirut. They also met my parents for the first time.

Other visitors that we welcomed in our house were Thomas and Hermine Schellen, a Blessed couple sent as missionaries to Lebanon, and their two kids Natasha and Sergé. They stayed with us for two months until they found their own place. The Schellens stayed in Lebanon as missionaries, and their children attended Lebanese schools and grew up in Lebanon. They truly dedicated their life to Lebanon and contributed enormously to the church activities there.

Larry

In the middle of the year, I found out that I was pregnant. This time my parents were there to help, especially my mom. She dedicated every weekend to come by and cook delicious meals for the whole week. My parents were so delighted to spend precious time with the grandkids. We celebrated Christmas and the children's birthdays together for the first time. I was so inspired to be able to catch up with my friends and cousins that I grew up with and share quality time together.

However, for Larry it wasn't as easy as living in Cairo. There weren't many expatriates in Lebanon as the country was recovering from fifteen years of civil war, which had devastated its economy and paralyzed its tourism. Besides, the Lebanese people spoke more French than English so Larry didn't have so many friends to talk with.

One day, Larry got sick. He had a fever and a bad cough, so I called the doctor who came to our home for a checkup. He found out that Larry had bronchitis, but he also noticed a heart murmur so he asked Larry to have his heart checked when he recovered.

Within two weeks, we scheduled an appointment with a heart doctor at Rizk Hospital in Ashrafieh, which was near to my parents' house. We found out that Larry had had a valve defect since birth that he didn't know about. Fortunately, it wasn't immediately critical, but the doctor told us that probably within a few years Larry would need to have open heart surgery to replace the valve. This was shocking news, and with this new health issue surfacing, and being pregnant with my fourth child, we started reflecting upon the next step in our life.

Larry's Father

Larry decided to call his parents in California to let them know about his heart condition, but no one answered. He tried again two days later. Still, no one was home so he called his sister, who told him that his parents were visiting Texas for a vacation and she would let them know about his call. Then a big surprise awaited us. While Larry's parents were vacationing in San Antonio, Texas, Larry's father, who was newly retired, had a heart attack and died in the hotel. When we heard the news, Larry got a ticket and flew to California to be with his mom and sister. It was devastating news. Suddenly Larry was dealing with the loss of his father at 66 years of age and his own heart condition.

When he came back home to Lebanon, he shared with me about his desire to move to the States for good. That way he could follow up with his heart condition and at the same time live near to his mom, who had lost her husband unexpectedly and her son to cancer many years ago.

Our Fourth Child

After giving birth to three children in Egypt, I gave birth to my fourth child, Scott, in Lebanon, on May 1,1997. Although my pregnancy with Scott was peaceful, the delivery was very hard.

My Lebanese doctor had advised me to schedule a day around my due time and take a pill to induce my labor. His explanation was that as a thirty-seven-year-old woman, I should not take any risk. Besides, our home was far from the hospital and there was always a traffic jam. The pill accelerated the pain in a way that I felt like my back was almost going to break. It even made it worse than a normal delivery, especially because the baby was much bigger than the previous ones.

Having Scott born in Lebanon was such a joyful occasion for my parents. My mother helped a lot and I was very much surrounded by family and relatives. It was the opposite of the time in Egypt when I gave birth to one child after the other without having any help, except for with Donald when my mother stayed with me for one month.

Scott was a happy boy, very content and easy going. He enjoyed all the activities around him and grew stronger and healthier every day. He was the one who received so much love and attention because we were surrounded by my family and relatives. But this didn't last for long, as we decided to move to the States.

Preparing to Leave

Although Scott was a very peaceful and easy baby, it was hard to take care of four kids when the eldest was only five. So, when we decided to move back to the States, Larry suggested he take Donald with him and go first and look for a job, find a place to live, and then I would follow him with the other children. Within two months of Scott's birth, Larry left with Donald and stayed at his mother's house until he found a job.

While Larry was in the States and we were planning to follow him later, I realized that I needed to apply for a passport for Scott. The American embassy had moved out of Lebanon during the war so I needed to go to Syria. In the Middle East, children follow their father's nationality and it doesn't matter where they were born or who the mother was. I called the embassy in Damascus and scheduled an appointment. Then I took baby Scott in a taxi early one morning to cross the border to Syria. At that time, Lebanon and Syria were on good terms and the borders were safe. My mother came to stay with Anne and Paul.

The trip was less than a three hours' drive. We left around 6 a.m. in order to avoid the traffic and arrive on time, but, unfortunately, we were stopped at the border. The Syrian army started questioning me and demanding proof that the baby was mine. I showed them the birth certificate, but still they didn't let me go until a couple of hours later when I was able to meet with one of the generals there and I explained my situation. He gave an order to let me go. It was a nerve-racking situation.

Finally, we arrived at the embassy in the late afternoon to find it closed. I decided to stay in a hotel and go the next day. As I explained my situation to the American consul the next morning, he smiled and told me to not worry, they would take care of Scott's papers and they would send me his passport by mail. I went back home thanking God that everything went well after all the troubles at the border, and that Scott would get his American ID. As we waited to join Larry and Donald in California as soon as Larry found a job and a place to stay, I enjoyed quality time with my beautiful mom, who was a real support for me during this time.

Callifornia

Four months after Larry and Donald left for the States, I packed and traveled with Anne, Paul, and six-month-old baby Scott. Saying goodbye to my parents was a heartbreaking experience as we truly didn't know when we would see each other again.

We arrived in California on October 31, 1997, Halloween night. Larry picked us up and drove us to Sunnyvale to have dinner with his mom. Then we headed to Hayward where Larry had rented an apartment for us to live in. Donald was so happy to see us after so many months alone with his father and his grandma.

After a two-month search, Larry had found a job at Stanford University. One day Fouad, a Palestinian immigrant whose mother was working as a secretary for the Methodist Church that Larry's parents attended, brought Larry a community newspaper which had ads for jobs. As Larry was checking it, he found an ad from Stanford University seeking administrative assistants. He mailed in his resumé, and it attracted the eye of a biology professor, who called Larry to schedule an interview. The professor, who was from a Jewish background and originally from Australia, was impressed by Larry's experience—Larry had worked for a few years at the *New York City Tribune in the United States, at the Middle East Times newspaper in Egypt, and* at the *Eco News in Lebanon. Also, he had two years' experience as an* administrative assistant at the American University in Cairo. This professor offered him the job as his assistant. Although the salary was small, they gave great benefits: medical insurance for all the family and full coverage of the children's tuition when they attended college. No one had expected that Larry would work at Stanford University, especially because he didn't have a college degree, so it was a big surprise for his family.

Our apartment in Hayward was affordable, compared to where grandma lived which was quite expensive. Also, it was close to our Bay Area Family Church, where Larry had enrolled Donald in the Principal Academy school, which was directed by our church members. But as time went by, it became a long commute for Larry to go back and forth to Stanford every day.

The first obstacle we faced was that I didn't drive. Somehow, I didn't feel the need to learn when I was in the Middle East. Maybe that was because the public transportation there was cheap and practical. But, in California, I was stuck with the children all day long while Larry went to work in the morning and came back in the evening.

I was happy to find one Blessed family in our building, Michael and Monika Kellett. They helped us by taking Donald to school. An interesting experience that I had at that time was meeting Monika's neighbor, a

European woman. We became good friends and despite having left that neighborhood twenty years ago, with everyone going to different places, we have kept connected by writing to each other until now.

Although we lived in Hayward for only three months, a few unusual accidents happened. One day when Larry took the kids to McDonald's, Anne fell down on the playground and cut her chin and got stitches. Less than one month after that accident, when I took the children to a park beside our apartment, Paul fell down and hurt his chin and got stitches the same as Anne. That was a weird coincidence and an interesting new beginning in the United States.

Our Fifth Child

With every new place to which we moved, a child came as a blessing that God bestowed on us in that place. In November of that year, I found out that I was pregnant. It was a surprise for us and for Larry's family, who were helping us to settle down. Grandma was very worried about how we were going to take care of our big family with Larry's limited income. She decided to get us a house in Sunnyvale to live near to her and to have more space for our growing family. But at the same time, she told us that we need to pay her a little rent and we needed to be responsible about all our expenses from now on. We were very excited to move to a house and it made the commute to Stanford University much easier and quicker for Larry.

In January 1998, we moved to Sunnyvale and we enrolled Donald in Vargas, a public elementary school. It was a nice coincidence to find out that because there was a railroad nearby, a school bus came every morning just in front of our house to pick up the kids and bring them back. It helped tremendously because I still wasn't driving yet.

The new beginning in Sunnyvale, and being pregnant with my fifth child, was an enormous task to bear. Although we had a house and Larry had a job, I was completely alone taking care of four kids under six years old, being pregnant, not driving, and not knowing anyone other than Larry's mother and sister. I didn't have any help and Larry's income was very little when he started so we were very tight financially, living on a monthly paycheck. The only place that I could take the children was a small park that was walking distance from our house. There the children would play in the playground and interact with the other kids their age. There also I met a neighbor, Marcela, and from that time we started a close friendship that continues today. She stood with me through thick and thin, and she was a source of joy and comfort whenever I needed it.

Reaching out to my neighbors was the best endeavor that I did for the first five years in California. I started inviting mothers whose children were the same age as mine. In this way, we got to know each other while we were sharing a cup of coffee and while the children were playing and having fun. Although it was overwhelming sometimes, it was worth doing it. I started getting to know my neighbors and building lasting relationships.

The time finally came to give birth to my fifth child. I remember vividly when I found out that I would have a girl, how happy and excited I was, telling all my neighbors and friends that I would have a girl. I never minded in the past what gender my baby would be, except for this time. I truly wanted a sister for Anne because I never had a sister myself, and deep in my heart I always felt that sisters carry their mother's heart when the mother is no more with them.

God answered my prayers and on July 20, 1998 Helen Hanna was born in Santa Clara, California at Kaiser hospital. It was a very painful and difficult delivery as fluid was blocking the baby from coming out. I was surprised that my regular doctor didn't show up and the baby was delivered by a nurse practitioner. I remember saying to Larry, who attended all my deliveries, that the pain was unbearable. But after the delivery, seeing sweet Helen looking at me, a healthy and happy baby, made me forget the world and all the pain that I had encountered during the delivery.

My sister-in-law took care of the children while I was in the hospital. When I brought Helen home, the children were so excited to meet their baby sister. It was again a new beginning for our growing family here in California. We named her Helen Hanna after my mother and my grandmother. As Scott was around one year and three months old when Helen was born, I needed to pay attention to both of them at the same time like raising twins.

Helen was a strong and healthy girl, full of life and excitement. She never wanted to be left alone. She always wanted to participate in all the activities that her siblings were doing. She had a very strong will, and since her childhood she loved to compete and win. The hardest thing for me at that time was lacking sleep. As Helen used to wake up many times at night, and I needed to take care of the children the next day, I was never able to take a nap. I remember how many times while sitting in the backyard watching the children playing, the tears would roll down my cheeks, feeling lonely and helpless; no one to visit, no one to talk to. I became very sensitive to the little things around me, like looking at the beautiful pink flowers blooming in our yard, or a butterfly passing by. It gave me a lot of comfort in that time and it helped me to feel God's love embracing me and watching over my kids.

THIRTEEN

A Working Mother

Raising a big family with one income in a high technology place was a big challenge. It was difficult to pay the rent to Grandma Bond, even though it was very little. Any time something broke down in the house, like the washing machine or the water heater, we couldn't afford to fix it. It was very hard on Larry to ask his mom for help each time as she had warned us that we should take full responsibility for our finances and not keep depending on her.

With this reality, I needed to step up and help Larry to pay the bills. The first obstacle was that I didn't drive, and I didn't have the time to learn as I had just had a new baby and all my children were very young. So, any work that I intended to do, Larry had to take me and bring me back, as well bring the children along because they were too young to be left by themselves. Another obstacle was that I couldn't work during the week because Larry had a full-time job, so I needed to work either nights or weekends.

One day when we were attending Sunday service at our church in San Leandro, I heard Hiroko Melosh, a Japanese sister who lived in a nearby city, saying that her mother-in-law was looking for a caregiver for her father-in-law. Although I had never had any experience in taking care of the elderly and it was by any means a very humble job, I was determined to help Larry and take responsibility for my family. I went to see Grandma Melosh, who showed me what to do—from bathing the old man to feeding him and taking him for a walk outdoors. I remember how much I cried at that time. Although I was put in a servant position, nevertheless, I was determined to work any job in order to not beg for money. The Melosh family was very happy to have me so I started going every weekend while Larry took care of the children.

Despite the hardships at that time, our family became closer, sharing more quality time and bonding together. Each time Larry took the children out, he tried to find a new park, a new playground, a new McDonald's, and any new place to entertain them. He used to play with them by pretending that he was a "Monster" going after them, and you would see all the kids in the park running after him. I was so thankful to have such a wonderful husband and a wonderful father for my kids. Both of us tried very hard to support each other and to share the load. Within six months, the old man's health deteriorated, so he went to a nursing home and my work ended.

Meanwhile, Anne started going to school with Donald and Paul followed her the next year, so I started looking for a better job.

My second job was at Michaels art store. When I found out that they were hiring, I applied for three days a week: one evening during the week and the whole weekend. Although it was a simple job, stacking and organizing the shelves with all kinds of decorations and art materials, I enjoyed it. I started buying nice decorations for my house, especially for the holidays.

For the first five years in California, we rarely went anywhere other than work and home with the children, except in the summer. Then we got to participate in a family camp organized by our church where Blessed families got together and spent three to four days together in nature, sharing good time and creating good memories.

Heart Surgery

After we came back to the States, Larry followed up with his heart condition. We were very blessed that his work at Stanford had provided medical insurance for him and for all the members of his family. So, although his income was small, his work benefits were great. In the middle of 2001, when Larry went for a regular checkup for his heart, the doctor told him that it was time to do the open-heart surgery. His valve had started deteriorating so he needed to replace it with a mechanical valve.

At that time, my eldest child was 9 years old and my youngest was only 3. I asked my friends Marcela, Heike, and Paula to take care of my children while I was with Larry in the hospital. Also, my sister-in-law Debbie and her husband Ted helped as well. On June 6, Ted took grandma, Larry, and myself to the San Francisco hospital where Larry underwent open heart surgery, which took approximately eight hours. I remember how calm Larry was when they took him to the operating room; the opposite of myself who was shaking. My heart wanted to jump out of my chest and just be there with him in the operating room.

While waiting for him in the lobby, his mom and his brother-in-law went for lunch, but I couldn't eat or sit or go anywhere. I just stood beside the operating room, praying all the time. Finally, the nurse approached me and told me that I could come and see him now. I went with his mom to the ICU room where he was hooked up with all the medical wires to monitor his heart. As soon as he saw us, he looked at me and whispered "I love you." Tears came down my cheeks like a river. I couldn't talk or say anything, I just sat quietly beside him and put my hand on his hand. I didn't want to leave him alone in his room. I absolutely didn't want to go back home until I had made sure that he was out of danger. So, I stayed there all night. I was surprised how the hospital was completely empty at night except for the nurses and the patients. I heard later that it was uncommon for family members to stay overnight.

The next day, Larry was out of the ICU and the nurses were encouraging him to start walking a few steps at a time. On the third day, they sent him home and his doctor warned him that no one should approach him as his chest was all stitched and so he should be extra careful. Larry decided instead of coming home to go to his mom's house, because our young kids, Scott and Helen, four years and three years old at that time, were used to jumping and climbing on him as soon as they saw him. It would be hard for them to understand the seriousness of his situation.

Although it was the right decision, it broke my heart because I really wanted to watch over Larry and take good care of him. Besides, staying at his mom's house meant that every time I visited him, someone needed to stay with the kids and someone needed to drive me there. We cried every time we met, we felt very hopeless. I was so worried about him, if he needed anything in the middle of the night. But God was truly on our side and within a few weeks, he recovered and came back home safe and sound.

I remember seeing True Mother in my dream around that time. She came and gave me a big hug.

Different Challenges and Different Jobs

As the children started going to school one after the other, I realized that it was time to learn to drive. I was in my early forties so it was hard. I failed the driving test twice, but I kept persevering until I passed. It took me a while to know about the directions and addresses and locations, and I never could overcome my fear of driving on the highways.

I remember in my first year of driving I had a very difficult experience. One day, Paul, Scott, and Helen wanted to go to the library, so I dropped them off and went to the laundromat. While I was doing my laundry, I realized that the library closed early on the weekend so I rushed to pick up the kids. On my way back, I took a wrong exit and somehow I ended up in a different city. Meanwhile the library closed and the children were waiting outside all alone. At that time, I didn't have a cellphone to contact Larry. After waiting for some time, Paul went to the public phone and dialed 911. When I arrived at the library, no one was there so I went home feeling hysterical to find a policeman standing at my front door with my children. I tried to explain what had happened, worrying about the consequences, but the policeman was very kind and he commended Paul for taking responsibility for his siblings. Although nothing happened, I felt so guilty and frustrated for many days.

Another similar story happened one day while I was with the kids at the nearby park. One of my little ones needed a change so instead of bringing all of them back home, I just took the two youngest and left the others playing in the playground. When I came back, a policeman was waiting for me. He told me that I should never leave the children unattended. I was so embarrassed and hurt because our house was very close nearby and it took me only 10 minutes to come back to them. It was hard for me to do everything by myself without any help.

My third job was working at the dollar store. As I was shopping there one day I met the owner, who was from Pakistan. He told me that he was looking for someone who he could trust to manage his store because he had a different job. The store was closer to my house and had better hours than Michaels, so I told him that I would like to try. I started managing the store all by myself, from organizing the shelves, to answering the phone calls, and standing as a cashier. Unfortunately, I couldn't continue there for very long because I faced an unusual situation. The store was located beside a high school. The high schoolers would pass by and just hang around in the store for fun. Then, through the security camera, I started seeing some of them stealing little items and putting them in their pockets. It was hard for me to handle the situation all by myself, so I quit.

As I tried to figure out what to do, I heard one neighbor talking about her friend looking for someone to babysit her twin girls in the morning for six months, until they started kindergarten. Although I was tired of taking care of kids and I preferred doing a different job, it was convenient as the family lived in my neighborhood, so I reached out to them.

I started going every morning to their house while my children went to school.

Another neighbor heard that I babysat, so after I finished babysitting these girls, she visited me and asked me if I could take care of her kids in my house. The mother was a native Palestinian married to an American and had two toddlers, a boy and a girl. She started bringing her kids to my house every morning around 7:30 and sometimes even at 7 a.m., because she had a deli restaurant where she prepared sandwiches early for her customers. It was hard on me as I needed to prepare my kids to send them to school and at the same time had additional kids to take care of. I compromised a lot in those days in order to provide my children with all the necessities.

Preschool Teacher

After trying different kinds of jobs, I ended up working for 12 years as a part-time preschool teacher in the city of Sunnyvale. Despite it never having been my specialty, or my major, to work with kids, and despite being already tired from raising a big family, nevertheless I tried my best to enjoy them and create a nice atmosphere for them. I did a lot of art and crafts with them as well as singing, dancing, and acting. I even tried inventing new ideas for them. One time we had an exhibition where we invited the parents to see their kids' art work. Another time, we created a new game where the children pretended that they were pirates and they needed to look for the treasure by learning how to use a map.

By working at the preschool, I came to meet families who came from different backgrounds: Mexican families, Asians, people from India, and so forth. It was a fascinating experience for me to come to know differ-ent traditions and cultures. It opened my eyes and touched my heart, and taught me to embrace all kinds of people as family members. After all, we need to learn from the children that they don't distinguish the differences. They play all together regardless of their skin color, their eth-nicities, or their beliefs. Many times, when the grandparents came to visit from different states, you could see the kids excited to bring them to their class to meet their friends.

That's what made my work at the preschool more meaningful because I came to meet people from all around the world. I even kept friendships with some of them after they moved out of the city. One preschooler whose family is from Zimbabwe kept sending me letters after she moved with her family to Gilroy, which is an hour's drive from my city. She is now a high schooler, and just recently I passed by her city and I went and visited her.

Some years I juggled two jobs at the same time. Like when I did yard duty at my daughter's school where I watched the children during lunch break. Also, I babysit an Indian toddler named Akash in the after-noons. The young parents were from India but they grew up in the United States. I became good friends with Priya, Akash's mom, and despite them moving to Texas, we kept calling each other and staying in touch, even exchanging gifts. Through my work, I built a deep friendship and an ever-lasting relationship.

FOURTEEN

A Lasting Friendship

When I think back on my first years in California, one of my favorite encounters was with an English grandma who was visiting her son. One day, Shirley was taking her grandson to the park when they passed by my house and stopped when they saw my youngest kids playing in the front yard. We started talking to each other, and I invited her and her grandkid to come inside. She visited me a few times and we shared teatime together. She went back to England after she spent one month in California. I saw her again the following year for the last time as her son and his family moved to a different state. On Christmas of that year, Shirley sent me a lovely Christmas card saying, "Tell Larry that I have an extra bed for you and him if you ever visit England." I kept this card in my drawer throughout the years as a reminder of my old friend from England.

Another lovely memory was when a new neighbor moved to our street. They were a young couple, Chris and Carien. The husband was American and the wife was Dutch. When Carien's parents came from Holland to visit their daughter, we invited them for dinner in our house to welcome them. Since then, every Christmas they send us delicious Dutch chocolate. And now, despite their daughter having moved to Boston, we still receive a Christmas card from them every year.

These neighbors became like a family to me. When Manijeh and Hassan next door heard that I was sending money to my mom, they offered a donation. And when Heidi down the street heard that I was planning to become an American citizen, she offered to pay the entire fee for me. A similar thing happened with another neighbor couple, Heidi and Nik. When Nik passed away, Heidi offered me a thousand dollars, and told me that she and Nik had always wanted to help me with the expense of becoming an American citizen.

Also two church friends , Heiki and Hiroko, became a big support for me as they stood by my side and whenever I needed help, they offer their support. One day Heiki introduced me to her Greek neighbor Paula, who started visiting me often and giving me a hand whenever I needed. She was like a sister to me and since then we became best friends.

Today I am standing on the foundation of all these friendships.

Lessons to Learn

It took me five years to really feel at home in California. I learned many things the hard way. For example, if I don't ask for help, no one will offer it. I always felt that it was obvious that I needed help, but here people are always busy and they don't like to be disturbed. So, everyone needs to depend on themselves. For a long time, I felt very lonely. No one was visiting and no one was even calling.

In the beginning, and as a newcomer, listening to the news made me so anxious. I used to hear all the time about children being kidnapped, so I worried that someone might hide behind a bush and kidnap one of my children.

Receiving random phone calls was also a new adjustment. People called asking for donations, like for the cancer society or for city police officers. It was something new for me, and I didn't know what to say and how to handle it. So, I always ended up donating in a time when we were living on a monthly paycheck and we needed help ourselves.

The biggest adjustment was when the children were invited for sleepovers at their friend's house. It was very uncommon in my culture. Besides, I didn't know the families! Some of them were single mothers who had boyfriends. I tried to meet the parents and tell them exactly about our family values and ask them very sincerely to stick to those values when my children were visiting them.

Another challenging experience was when the children were going to a school camp. In 5th grade the school organizes a one-week camp. For 10-year-olds to be far from home with schoolmates and teachers for the entire week is kind of harsh in my opinion. I also struggled a lot when my kids were camping, sleeping in a tent in a place where there were bears around. All that made me worried and not able to rest until they were back home.

Becoming a Part of the Community

Year by year, I learned to cope in my new home and overcome the challenges that I faced in my daily life. Because we lived far from our church, we started attending the local Methodist Church, Larry's parents' church. Larry joined his mom singing in the choir and he did it for over 20 years. I tried to be involved in the church by giving Sunday Service for the children, as well supporting the Methodist women's activities like helping with rummage sales and holiday events for kids.

One of the things that I loved to do while I was adjusting to my new home was reading the biographies of the Presidents of the United States. I always loved history and reading about the lives of the leaders who left their mark in history. It really helped me to love my new country. Sometimes I used to see the presidents in my dreams. Even when I was growing up in Lebanon, I remember seeing President Bashir El Gemayel in my dream after he was assassinated. I saw his daughter, who was killed a few years before him, holding his hand and showing him the way to my house. One time, after 9/11, I decided to send a Christmas card to the White House, telling the First Lady Laura Bush that I was praying for the President and the country. To my surprise, she answered me with a nice letter coming directly from the White House. And the following year, I received a letter coming from the office of President George W. Bush. Although it is generally the staff of the White House who reply, still I felt connected to the providence of the country.

My house was always in a festive mood. Five kids meant five birthday celebrations with family and friends. Also, we celebrated the holidays and anniversaries. I always cooked big meals and invited Larry's family as well as the children's friends or my neighbors. Despite it being very tiring, I enjoyed every moment of it.

A Surprising Encounter

After coming to California, I read and watched many documentaries about the Presidents of the United States and the First Ladies, learning about their lives and how they climbed the ladder to the White House. I connected particularly with Ronald Reagan. His eternal optimism and his qualities as a great communicator left a big impression on me. One day, as we were visiting Larry's relatives in Santa Maria, we decided to go and visit the President Reagan Library at Simi Valley. We enjoyed touring Air Force One and the museum. When we stopped at the cafeteria there, something amazing happened.

While we were sitting enjoying lunch with the children, I heard people behind me in the adjoining booth talking in Arabic. I turned around and introduced myself as a native Lebanese. They were happy to meet me and I found out that they were also Lebanese and they lived in Los Angeles. The old man who was accompanying them looked at me and asked me who my father was. When I told him his name was Elias Akiki and he used to work as an accountant at Abou Adal's company, he opened his eyes wide and said, "Elie is your father?" Only my father's close friends used to call him Elie. I looked at my children in disbelief and I said, "He knew my father!" I never imagined that I would meet someone in the United States who would know my father. It was a rendezvous made in heaven.

FIFTEEN

A Special Year: 2006

Because of our financial situation, as well as our big family, I couldn't visit Lebanon often. That caused me great agony. I literally sacrificed my parents. I didn't have a choice. I felt so sorry for my mom who loved me and missed me dearly. It took me five years to go and visit my parents after we came to the States. My first visit back to Lebanon was in 2002. I went by myself for two weeks while Larry took care of the kids. Then in June 2006, I heard that my mother had become sick and went to the hospital. It was a wakeup call. Despite our financial challenges, I decided to go and take my two daughters with me.

I contacted the National Leader of Lebanon, Thomas Schellen, to tell him about my intention to visit Lebanon. He was very surprised and told me that True Mother was visiting Lebanon at that time in her tour of the Middle East. He would appreciate any help bringing more audience to the event. I was very excited to be able to see my mom and at the same time welcome True Mother to Lebanon together with my daughters.

My parents were very happy to see us and specially to see Anne and Helen. Anne was only four years old when we left Lebanon in 1997, so she didn't remember much, and Helen was born in the States so my parents had never seen her before. We enjoyed quality time with my family and, at the same time, we joined brothers and sisters who came from the Middle East region, from Japan, and some from Europe as well to help Thomas and Hermine prepare for True Mother's event.

At that time, Alfred was already back in Lebanon and was living in South Lebanon near to his family and relatives, so he invited all his relatives and contacts to the event. I tried to do the same with the time limit that I had. I contacted my cousins and my friends as well as my neighbors. As the event approached, each one of the members who were helping was given a list of Lebanese VIPs to contact and to invite.

Among the names on my list was a young politician named Pierre Gemayel, who was the son of the former President Amin Gemayel and the nephew of the late President Bashir Gemayel, who was assassinated after taking office. I remember how much I cried when I heard about the assassination. A lot of people did. When I called the office of Mr. Gemayel, who was the Minister of Industry at that time, I was lucky that he answered the phone directly. He was very polite and respectful. I told him that I was coming all the way from California to invite him. He laughed and thanked me. But he apologized that he could not make it because he was going out of the country, but he promised to send a delegation to represent him.

True Mother came with Kook Jin-nim and his wife as well as True Parents' youngest daughter. Both Anne and Helen as well Thomas' children,

Natasha and Sergé, offered True Mother and True Children flowers on their arrival at the hotel. The event went very well with around 700 people attending. I brought my mother and my brothers, and some of my cousins and friends came as well. The same as in Egypt, I was asked to go on stage and offer True Mother a pair of porcelain bluebirds this time, instead of flowers. Toward the end of the event, the members and the Ambassadors for Peace came to the stage to take a memorable picture with True Mother. I rushed up to the audience and picked up my mother and took her to the stage. I felt strongly that she deserved to be up there with our beloved True Mother. I stood up very proudly on the same stage with my own mother and our beloved True Mother. That was a memorable experience for me as the first sister who joined in Lebanon.

As we were planning to go home after the event, one Japanese brother approached me and offered me and my daughters a room in the hotel where True Mother was staying. I was so touched by his offer and I felt God's love for me as the first Lebanese sister to join. Next morning, I participated in morning prayer with our True Mother. After the prayer, True Mother asked the members what they thought about the event. Alfred stood up and reported to True Mother about all the delegations who came from different parts of Lebanon representing different religious and traditional backgrounds. Then I stood up and said something like, "The Lebanese people seek beauty and ideals. By attending the event, they found it in True Mother who moved everyone's heart."

True Mother encouraged us to teach the Divine Principle not only to the Lebanese people but to the Middle Eastern people as well. She said Lebanon throughout history was a mediator between the West and the

Arabs. Therefore, the Lebanese should bring the Arabs to True Parents.

Within a few hours, we said goodbye to True Mother, wishing her a safe trip on her tour in the Middle East and we went back to my parents' house to stay for another week. That week, we went and visited my relatives in Baskinta and we stayed at Maguy's house for the weekend, enjoying time with my cousin and her family, picking cherries from her garden, eating fresh eggs, and going for a long walk in nature.

Time passed quickly and it was never easy to say goodbye to my parents. Nevertheless, we created beautiful memories to cherish for the rest of our lives.

A Second Opportunity

Within a few months after coming back from Lebanon, I received a phone call from our pastor Kevin Thompson asking me if I could assist the American Clergy who were going to Lebanon on their Middle East tour. True Parents have been promoting dialogue between the different religions and denominations throughout their entire life. In the Middle East, they were promoting dialogue and reconciliation between Christians, Muslims, and Jews, the three Abrahamic faiths. It was quite a surprise and such an opportunity to be able to help. I was tremendously thankful to Larry for taking care of the children again so I would be able to travel.

At the beginning of November 2006, I traveled together with Wafaa, a Jordanian Ambassador for Peace, who has been a big support and a wonderful friend to our church. We went through Heathrow Airport, where we waited a few hours to take our next flight to Beirut. It was an interesting experience to travel with Wafaa. She was equipped with all kinds of food and drinks and even medicine, so we didn't need to buy anything on our way. We just had a feast at the airport and enjoyed each other's company. I learned by accompanying Wafaa that if I ever travel with a Middle Eastern friend, I will never get hungry.

Another interesting experience I had while we were traveling was when a minister came on board and sat a few seats in front of us. I could hear him talking to the young Lebanese man who was sitting beside him. After introducing himself, he just started directly talking about the purpose of his visit to Lebanon and that's how I found out that he was one of the clergymen who were sent to Lebanon by our church. I heard him saying something like, "Do you know who's sending me to Lebanon? Do you know Rev. Moon of the Unification Church? He is the man who's sending me to promote peace and dialogue between the different denominations in your country." He really was speaking with a lot of authority. The young man was nodding all the time and listening carefully to his religious companion. I learned a lot from this pastor even before we got together in Lebanon. I understood deeply the role of the clergy in promoting peace and harmony in the world.

As we arrived in Beirut, I started feeling sick. I developed a heavy cough and shivers. Wafaa gave me medicine for the cold and I went directly to sleep. I stayed in bed the next day until the evening when I joined Wafaa to welcome all the ministers who came from the States. Dr. Yang and Rev. Michael Jenkins were representing our church, Rev. Jesse Edwards representing the American Clergy, and around 10 American pastors were gathered. Also, we welcomed the Lebanese religious figures from Christian and Muslim backgrounds.

The next day, we attended an orientation gathering where each member of our church was assigned to accompany a minister to visit public and religious figures in the country. I was happy to accompany an American clergy couple, who were the only couple among the ministers who came together to Lebanon from the States. They truly represented the parental figures of our beloved True Parents.

Our first visit was to a community college where the principal was an Ambassador for Peace. The minister was given the chance to talk to one of the classes on the topic of inter-religious dialogue. The students were very receptive and attentive to what the American clergyman had to say. He really encouraged them to overcome all the divisions that war has created and to reach out to each other as Lebanese citizens beyond their affiliation to their religion or their political connections. He also told them that peace doesn't start from top to bottom but, on the contrary, it starts from the individual to the family until it reaches the leadership.

The next day, we went to visit a politician who had attended one of our conferences in Europe. His wife prepared a delicious meal for us and she also invited a few guests to meet us. The minister offered them the holy wine and blessed them. Then he offered a sincere prayer asking God to guide this politician to serve his people and his country with honesty and a good example. As we were leaving, the American pastor turned to the Lebanese politician, shook his hand and told him that the best leader to follow is our own conscience because God resides in it.

For the next few days, some of the ministers went to visit the Lebanese parliament while others visited religious figures, where they introduced the work of Rev. Moon in building a network of inter-religious dialogue and an interfaith global foundation. The week passed quickly, and I didn't have a chance to visit my parents. Wafaa went to visit her relatives in Jordan, and I headed to the airport by myself to fly back to the States.

For some reason the airport was overcrowded and almost chaotic. The security lines were very long, and the process was very slow, which led me to miss my flight for the first time in my life. I contacted Larry to let him know, and I rescheduled my flight and then went back home to stay for two days with my parents. It was a nice surprise for them to see me again, and it gave me quality time to spend with my father for the last time, as he passed away a few months after my visit. God must have had a plan to let me stay those two more days.

Another interesting experience I encountered on my way back to California was while I was waiting for my next flight from Heathrow Airport I heard an announcement on the TV that Mr. Pierre Gemayel had been assassinated. The young Gemayel that I had talked with on the phone and invited to True Mother's event just a few months ago had been killed. I was in disbelief, and the tears started running down my cheeks. I ran to catch my second flight and this time instead of having Wafaa to travel with, the spirit and the voice of Mr. Gemayel accompanied me home.

My two cousins and close childhood friends, Nada and Maguy, together with our neighbor Silva.

Our family in 1998, with newborn daughter Helen.

My neighbors and friends in Sunnyvale, from left to right, Heike, Heidi, Manijeh, Parivash, myself, Marcela, and Paula.

My church friends Heike Parkin and Hiroko Melosh.

*Myself with a Druze couple, attending
a church conference in Lebanon, 2006.*

*Accompanying American pastors visiting Lebanon with our church leaders
Rev. Michael Jenkins and Rev. Yang, 2006.*

With my brother Ibrahim in Lebanon, 2013.

Representing the Women's Federation for World Peace,
in Sunnyvale, California.

With my husband and children in Sunnyvale, California, 2015.

Larry and I in Sunnyvale, California, 2015.

SIXTEEN

Saying Goodbye

My father passed away in 2007, within a few months after my visit, so I couldn't attend his funeral. Instead, I went back to Lebanon in 2008 for his one-year anniversary. I saw my father in my dreams many times after he passed. In one of my dreams, he was carefully showing me a few gemstones that he was holding in his hands. In another dream I saw him in a training camp, and I was there with three church members, my spiritual father Adel Jamati, the national leader of France Henri Blanchard, and Mr. Umberto Angelucci. As I was visiting him in the camp, I encouraged him to come inside and listen to Divine Principle lectures.

By then I realized that my mother was becoming old and fragile as well, and her time was also running out. I felt so guilty because I couldn't visit her very often. Our financial situation was very hard, and as our children were growing their demands were very high. It took me another five years to go back to Lebanon and visit my mom again in April 2013. It turned out to be the last time I saw her.

On this visit, my brother Ibrahim took us to visit Saint Charbel monastery. He was the Lebanese saint who had appeared to me in my dream when I was a teenager. As soon as I entered his temple, the tears started running down my cheeks uncontrollably. I was so surprised, and I tried to hide it from my mom so she would not worry about seeing me cry. I truly didn't have any reason to cry. It was kind of an overwhelming spiritual experience. On our way back home, we stopped at a nice restaurant in the city of Tripoli and we had fish for dinner. It was like my last supper together with my mom.

The next day, my flight was in the middle of the night so my mother couldn't stay awake. But she asked me to wake her up before I left. I entered her bedroom while she was sleeping and offered a full bow and knelt down beside her bed and prayed. I thanked her for all her unconditional love and support to me throughout the years. I asked her to forgive me for not being able to take care of her, then I went and kissed her goodbye. She woke up and screamed. It was as if she knew deep down in her heart that it could be our last hug.

Within ten months of my visit, in February 2014, my mom passed away. I waited to see her in my dream and she came. The dream was very meaningful. We were walking together in a very beautiful place, hugging each other and looking at the beautiful nature around us. I was telling her, "Look mom, how beautiful the waterfall is. Look mom, how lovely the mountains are, covered by the snow." We were united in one heart and one soul. The dream was a true expression of our relationship as mother and daughter. We were one in heart and soul.

Losing My Beloved Friend

Although diplomatic relations between Lebanon and Iran were unstable, Vera managed to convince the Iranian consulate to give her a visa to travel to Iran. She joined Ahmad almost three years after being Blessed in Korea. Ahmad was living with his family at that time. In order to live together and start their family, they participated in a Muslim wedding ceremony surrounded by Ahmad's parents and siblings.

Although Ahmad had studied electrical engineering, he couldn't find a job. Iran had a lot of sanctions at that time and the country was suffering from government corruption and misuse of power. So, after their daughter Sarah was born, they decided to move out of the country. They couldn't go to Lebanon because the country was still dealing with war and conflict. They decided to go to Korea, as they were able to obtain visas. They settled down there, although it was very hard for Ahmad to find a job as he didn't have a work permit. He did a couple of jobs in the church and Vera taught English at a local school. Two children were born in Korea, Arman and Mina.

Toward the end of September 2014, I received an unexpected phone call from Korea. It was Vera telling me that she had cancer, stage four ovarian cancer. The doctors gave her five years to live. It was shocking news. My beloved friend needed me. Oh God, please take care of Vera. I felt the urgency to go and see her. I packed and I went to Korea two weeks after hearing from her.

Vera didn't believe that I was coming. She waited eagerly to welcome me to her house. We hugged and we cried. We laughed and we wept. Her children were happy to meet me. Sarah played piano and Mina drew beautiful pictures for me. I stayed with them for two weeks. I accompanied Vera to her chemotherapy. I cooked lentil soup for her and shared Turkish coffee in the mornings, as we used to do in college. I went with her daughters to visit their school. Mina, the youngest, took me to the park and showed me around. I watched her son Arman playing soccer, and I went shopping with Ahmad. The days went quickly and soon it was time to say goodbye. We hugged again and we cried again. We waved goodbye and I promised to come and visit her again.

Within two months after my visit, Vera passed away. I couldn't fulfill my promise to go and visit her again. But I saw her in my dream. She was digging at the side of road and doing hard work when I met her. I asked her if she wanted to go back to her parents' house. She said no, let's go to the church center, this is my home. And we walked there together.

Vera and my mom, both of them my spiritual daughters, passed to the spiritual world in the same year, 2014.

Saying Goodbye to True Father

I met True Mother many times in my life but True Father only twice, In Korea during the Holy Marriage Blessing and in San Francisco during a conference in 2005. I went with Heike, my German friend, to attend morning devotion after attending the conference in San Francisco. We decided at the end of the reading and prayer to go to the back door of the hotel where True Parents were staying, and hoped to have a chance to say goodbye to them when they left. Most of the members had left and we were the only ones, with maybe two others, who were standing there. To our delight, True Parents came out and their driver met them at the back of the driveway. I rushed up with Heike to be closer to them and to wave goodbye. As they were getting into the car, I shouted loudly saying to them, "True Parents we love you, True Parents we love you!" They looked at us, smiled, and waved goodbye.

That was the last time that I saw True Father before he ascended to the spirit world. This memory will stay with me forever because I was able to express my love and gratitude to our beloved True Parents who blessed us and showed us the way to serve God and to serve humanity as one global family.

SEVENTEEN

A Love Story

My purpose in writing this book is to share my love story to God, our Heavenly Parent, to my parents who supported and trusted me, and to my people who, despite the war and the hardships, kept hope.

It's the story of a man of faith who kept knocking on doors until he found me, and how the journey led me to connect to True Parents, Rev. Sun Myung Moon and Mrs. Hak Ja Han Moon, whose main purpose is to fulfill God's dream in creating a world of peace starting from individuals to families, nations, and world.

It's a fascinating discovery of how God has been working through historical figures to bring humanity back to Him.

Finally, it's a story of true love between me and my husband, who decided together with other people of faith to sacrifice our own ambitions and to serve our fellow human beings in order for God's will to be done on earth as it is in heaven.

A Grateful Life

I grew up during the civil war in Lebanon and I am so grateful for God who protected me and my family during that time. I opened the door to Adel and welcomed him, and since then I am thankful to have been able to travel and connect to people from all around the world. I went to Korea and trusted that God had prepared a faithful man for me. I am eternally grateful to True Parents who blessed me with a wonderful man, and together we built a beautiful family centered upon good principles and values.

I served my husband and I served my children. I served my relatives and I served my neighbors. I loved my family and my ancestors, and I loved all kinds of people that I met: Indian, Chinese, Mexican, South American, and European. I found a friend in each one of them and I was a happy, positive person. I found goodness and forgot the ugliness. I found love and forgave the hurt. I celebrated holidays, birthdays, and anniversaries, and I wished everyone what I wished for myself and for my family. That's why I am forever grateful.

Simple acts

When I was growing up, I was always interested in making others feel happy by bringing them gifts and celebrating their birthdays. For example, in the building where I lived there was a poor Syrian family who had many kids. During Christmas time, as well as on some other occasions, I used to buy them a few things, ring the doorbell, leave the groceries in front of the door, and leave. Even my parents didn't know about that.

I did the same thing a few times when I found out about my friend Josephine's neighbor. When I went to visit her one day and we sat together on her balcony, I noticed an old lady was sitting on the other side across from us, knitting and watching the people going by. I asked my friend about her, and she told me that she was a widow and she lived all by herself. The next day, I went to the store and bought flowers and cookies and, as she kept her door unlocked, I snuck into her living room without her seeing me and put them on her table and left.

Since my youth, I really enjoyed doing something nice for others, just to uplift their spirits. I wasn't so much interested in giving money or doing charities, but mostly trying to change the circumstances by an act of kindness.

I remember in my village, when my mother used to ask me to get her some groceries, I would go and knock on my neighbor's house and ask her if she needed anything from the store as well.

At school, I used to bring a lot of gifts to my teachers to show them my appreciation and gratitude. One time, I took one of my mom's beautiful pins without even telling her and I gave it to my teacher on teacher's appreciation day. Of course, that wasn't the right thing to do, but at that time, I was so driven to make others feel happy and appreciated. It gave me a lot of satisfaction.

I carried this kind of characteristic into my adult life. Every time I hear someone's birthday is coming, it could be a neighbor or a friend, not only a family member, I will decorate my house and buy a cake and gifts and invite everyone to get together and enjoy celebrating that person's birthday. That's what really helped me to feel that I am at home when I moved to California, far from my family and my culture.

Life Lessons

Nature

Growing up surrounded by nature is the key for a beautiful childhood and lovely memories. Wherever we live, we need to make sure to go out in nature. Go to the hills and to the prairies. Walk on the beaches and watch the sunset. The best nutrition we can give to our children is to take them out in nature. It could be a day trip, or a weekend camping, or even an hour in the park. The freedom of being surrounded by trees and flowers, feeling the warmth of the sun on our shoulders, and the touch of the wind on our faces, will absolutely help us to find peace within ourselves and with others.

I grew up during the civil war in Lebanon, but because my parents took us to the village so often, the war didn't leave deep scars in our hearts. On the other hand, when we came to California, our finances were very limited and we needed to raise five children with a very tight income. We started going on picnics. At least twice a week, I used to wrap sandwiches, take some chips and drinks, and wait for Larry to find us a new park to explore each time. This helped us to bond together as a family and create good memories.

Friendship

From the beginning to the end, having friends makes life so colorful and beautiful.

The best gift we can offer to a child is not a toy or a treat, but to connect him or her to a playmate. How sad it will be if a child doesn't have a friend. Many times, parents focus upon their children's education and forget about their social skills. When we have friends, we learn to communicate, to express our feelings and emotions, to compromise, and to take turns.

When I worked as a preschool teacher, I noticed how important it was for kids not to be isolated but to be surrounded by schoolmates and friends so they could grow in a healthy atmosphere.

When I came to the United States, I found myself so alone, raising five children all by myself. I turned to my neighbors. I started inviting them for coffee. And day by day, we started opening our hearts to each other and sharing our thoughts and opinions. We became good friends. It benefited us and it benefited our children.

In Lebanon, I grew up with three friends, two of whom were my cousins. We have been good friends since childhood. The same with my neighbors in Beirut. We stayed connected for life. When I used to go to Lebanon to visit my parents, I couldn't not visit my neighbors as well as my cousins and friends. They were part of my family.

A true friend is the one who listens to you without judging you and will give you a hand even before you ask. Eventually your spouse becomes your best friend and your grown-up children become your closest friends.

Food is love

People can be generous with many things but real generosity comes from the heart. When we give money or material things people will thank us, but their hearts will be moved when we take time and care about them. Sharing a meal with a person will leave more of an impact on them.

When the gardener used to come to our house to mow the lawn, besides paying him for his work, I used to offer him a drink and fruits. I could see the difference on his face. He would sit and take time to rest and eat. He would show more gratitude for that than for the money that he worked for.

Sharing a meal with my neighbors and friends would bond us together. I always enjoyed inviting them to celebrate a birthday or an anniversary. I felt like I had the world sitting around my table because they were from different ethnicities and cultures. By serving them, my heart grew and my mind became universal.

In Lebanon, our neighbors will knock on our door and ask for a cup of rice or an egg whenever they need it. And whenever they have any extra food, they will be happy to share it with us. One of our next-door neighbors, Om Issam (the mother of Issam) used to bring us olive oil from her land in South Lebanon, and when my mother cooked a delicious meal, she would always share a dish with Om Issam.

Forgiveness

I found out through life experience that forgiveness means to not judge. We need to go beyond the hurt and try to understand why that person has been hurting us. We need to always take time to reflect and to heal. Forgiveness is absolutely not a one-time act; it is actually a process. That's why we need to try to place ourselves in the other person's shoes. But at the same time, we should not give them an excuse to hurt us.

From a young age, we need to teach our children not to hold grudges and not to go to bed being angry and resentful. That's why communication is important. Talk about what happened during the day and try to make a plan for how to solve the problem.

We need to also learn to forgive ourselves and our shortcomings. We need to realize that it's very important for our spirit and for our soul to live in peace and harmony by connecting to what makes us positive and leaving behind all the negativity and the hurt.

That's why in my book, I never wanted to talk about the people who hurt me. I never wanted to condemn them. I already forgave them, and I already moved on.

Prayer life

Prayer is so essential, like eating, drinking, and sleeping. Prayer doesn't mean just kneeling down, closing our eyes, and praying. It's more like a daily conversation within ourselves, reflecting, meditating, and eventually asking our creator to guide us in our endeavors. It's also a dialogue and a discussion even with our ancestors and relatives who are not with us anymore. Personally, I feel that my parents, who passed away many years ago, are always with me and I share with them my thoughts and feelings. Love never ends, and therefore prayer is a continuity of the love that we share with all our loved ones and ultimately our Heavenly Father.

Sometimes prayer means to report about our plans and ask God for guidance and protection. Personally, I always pray before I drive. Also, prayer reflects gratitude. In our home, we always pray before meals and we thank God for all the blessings that He bestowed on us.

Teaching children to pray helps them not to take things for granted and to be respectful and learn good manners in life.

"Joie de vivre"

Celebrate every day and enjoy living. Being positive brings good fortune. It's so interesting how poor people who don't have much in the way of material things can be happier than the rich people who have everything.

What really matters in life is to have the love of our family and the support of our friends, and everything else will be acquired gradually.

When I think about my people, the Lebanese people, despite the war and the collapse of the economy, they are always optimistic and believe in a better future. I remember how one house in our neighborhood got hit by a rocket during the civil war and how the following week the place was fixed, despite the fighting still going on.

No matter the situation, never give up hope and always find something to enjoy. In the end, what makes us happy is the love that we share and the memories that we create.

Unity

This word has a deep meaning. Unity makes us strong. A stick can be broken easily but a handful of sticks will be hard to break. Unity brings peace and harmony. I never wanted to cause any division. I truly treasured unity within the family, among friends, and mostly within myself.

I remember when we used to take our five children out and when we asked them which park they would like to go to, we would hear five different answers. And when we asked them to agree on one place, it was hard for them to unite. Can you imagine that the same five kids, now grown up, cannot agree about one place to meet or to get together! The parents would be devastated.

Unity means harmony. It also means agreement to put the purpose of the whole above the purpose of the individual.

Also, unity helps the family to be strong. Unity between husband and wife, between parents and children, as well between the siblings. One of the best compliments I received about my family was when I heard them saying, "You are the Bond family and you are truly bonding together."

God, the ultimate destination

How pitiful it is to hear that God does not exist! It's like looking at a beautiful work of art and saying, well it came about by chance because I didn't see the artist working on it.

By the same token, we should respect all the sages and the prophets who sacrificed in the past in order for us today to acknowledge the presence of the creator, and to work together for the sake of a harmonious and a peaceful world.

We should recognize True Parents, Rev. Sun Myung Moon and Dr. Hak Ja Han Moon, as parental figures who dedicated their entire lives to bring all denominations, all races and ethnicities to work together to fulfill God's dream on earth.

It's crucial for us who are living in this era to not miss this providential time, working together with our True Parents to build God's kingdom on earth. That's the dream of our ancestors in the past, it's our dream today, and it will be our future generations' dream as well.

Our ultimate destiny is to reach out to heaven and bring God to earth to live among us by building God-centered families and a God-centered world.

Do not miss what is important in life. God, family, and friends. We are created to receive love, to mature, and to share it and multiply it. Education and money are important tools, but they are not the goal in life. We are here for a reason. We are here to resemble the Creator who gave everything He has for His creation. We are the sons and daughters of

God, and one day we are going to join Him. What gifts shall we bring? Our love is the best gift to offer.

Amen.

Poems

I wrote this poem in 2006, after I accompanied the American pastors to Lebanon in their mission to encourage a peaceful dialogue between the different denominations which have been fighting each other for many years.

I also have a dream

I have a dream that one day we all shall live in peace

Muslims, Christians, and Jews, the three brothers will succeed

In accomplishing for their people very good deeds

And from heaven the face of Abraham,

the father of the three faiths will appear

Supporting their hard work and encouraging them to proceed.

I have a dream that one day I will visit Jerusalem

And I will stay one night in Tel Aviv

Then on my way back, I will bring a friend

And sail together into the Mediterranean Sea.

We will go to Egypt and visit the Pyramids

Then join a Nile cruise and pass by the Valley of the Kings

And before the sun goes down, we will stop by a mosque which is near

We will pray together and share a meal

Thanking God for the opportunity for our relationship to be healed.

We will continue to Turkey and visit Aya Sophia

Then go to Jordan and ride a camel in the Sahara Desert

I will insist to go to Beirut, the city which never sleeps

And offer my friend my favorite dishes and all kind of treats.

And while we are in Lebanon, I will take my friend to my village

And share with him my childhood stories while strolling
under the pine trees

I will make sure to visit my mom and sit together

enjoying the evening breeze

Then ask her to forgive me because I cannot stay as I please

My friend is in a hurry to go back home after a long trip around

the Mediterranean Sea.

Am I dreaming! Tell me, is it just a dream?

Yes, it was just a daydream.

But when we live in this land of the free

We hope that one day, peace will be achieved in the Middle East

And the dreams will become true and will have the chance

to be fulfilled, indeed.

I wrote this next poem after True Father,
Rev. Sun Myung Moon, died in 2012.

Let us love her the most

As the snow covers the head of the mountains

And the wind whispers in the ears of the valleys.

As the flowers bloom on the hands of the branches

Let us love her, side by side with nature.

She is here waiting

For a smile, for an act, for a prayer, she is waiting.

Like the fields full of seeds, waiting for the sunrise

And the sky full of stars, waiting for the moonrise.

She is here for you and me and for all the people whoever they are.

She is here waiting

For a smile, an act, a prayer, she is waiting.

Let us love her the most

Wipe her tears, make her smile.

Let us bring her back to our homes, to our hearts

And cherish her everywhere we go.

She is our dearest mother.

The True Mother of all humankind.

Proverbs from Lebanon

Daily proverbs

It is said in the Middle East that in every house there is either a musician or a poet, and for every occasion there is a proverb. The stories and the lessons that people have learned from their parents and grandparents for many generations created valuable quotes and advice to be shared. They also reflect the people's culture and their perspective on life.

Here are some of the proverbs that I heard from different people while I was growing up, which give an idea about the Lebanese mentality and their culture.

My mother use to say these proverbs so many times:

"Do good and throw it into the sea."

"The one whose hand is in fire is not like the one whose hand is in water."

"Only your nail scratches your skin."

My grandma who lived through World War II and raised her children in the village, used to say to us, her grandkids:

"Better to have one thousand enemies outside the house than to have one single enemy inside it."

In high school, my literature teacher told us on many occasions:

"Kids, time is gold so use it wisely."

Also, he used to say:

"If speaking is silver then silence is gold."

"Talking is not like doing."

In my village, when we used to get together with our neighbors and relatives, you would hear the old ladies saying:

"You will know your friends in times of need."

"Far from sight, far from the heart."

"When the angels arrive, the demons will leave."

"The monkey is a gazelle in the eyes of his mother."

Here are some proverbs that people say in their daily lives:

"Repetition teaches even the donkey," which means if you practice many times, you'll surely get it.

"If you are a gosling, you can swim," which means like father like son.

"Close the door that brings the wind and have peace," which means block whatever is causing you stress and relax.

"There is no sweetness without fire," which means nothing good comes easily.

"A pot finally found its own cover," meaning someone has found his perfect match.

"The eye can see but the hand is short," which means even if we find out what's going on, we might not be able to help.

"We went salad," meaning we've suffered a setback.

Recipes from Lebanon

Food is love and the Lebanese are generous by nature so whenever they have a guest, they will be treated like a king.

What makes Lebanese cooking healthy is all the lemon and garlic they add to it as well as the variety of dishes which combine beans, vegetables, and all kind of meat like beef, lamb, and chicken.

The following are recipes for my favorite Lebanese dishes, but in general I like most Lebanese foods like falafel, grape leaves, couscous with chopped almonds and pine nuts, as well all kinds of seafood.

Tabbouleh

A healthy Mediterranean appetizer made from parsley, tomatoes, bulgur wheat, lemon, and olive oil.

- First, soak a half cup of fine bulgur in a cup of water.

- Second, chop two bunches of Italian parsley very finely and soak them in water for 10 minutes to clean any dirt, then drain them.

- Then, dice three ripe tomatoes and add them to the parsley and drain the bulgur and add it as well.

- Then, squeeze two lemons into the dish and add three tablespoons of olive oil.

- Add salt and mix the ingredients very well and the tabbouleh is ready.

- Some people like to add a few pieces of chopped green onions or a few leaves of mint. Those are optional.

Hummus, my favorite dip

- Soak two cups of dried chickpeas in five cups of water overnight.

- Next day, boil them until they are very tender.

- In a food processor, add ⅓ cup of tahini to the cooked beans, two cloves of garlic peeled, one to two squeezed lemons, and one tablespoon of salt, ¼ cup of water, and blend all the ingredients together.

- The hummus can be eaten with pita bread or crackers and chips. Some people may prefer to have it with carrots, cucumbers, and celery.

- It's definitely a delicious and healthy dip.

Baba ghanouj

Another favorite and healthy dip. It consists of the same ingredients as the hummus dip except it uses eggplant instead of chickpeas.

- Place one large eggplant in the oven covered in foil and roast it for 40 minutes at 350 degrees.

- Then take it out of the foil and let it cool down completely before peeling it.

- Cut it into small pieces and place it in a food processor, add two tablespoons of tahini, one clove of garlic, one juiced lemon, salt and pepper, and blend it together for a short time. The eggplant is soft and it takes just a minute to mix in the blender.

- The same as hummus, you can eat it with pita bread or vegetables.

Za'atar

This dip might be very unfamiliar to people compared to hummus and baba ghanouj, but for me personally it is my favorite. It consists of only two ingredients, za'atar and olive oil.

Za'atar consists of a combination of dried oregano, thyme, and toasted sesame seeds. Mostly you eat it with pita bread as a dip. But in Lebanon, the bakeries prepare a yeasted dough as flat bread and bake it with za'atar and olive oil on top. It's called man'ousheh and it's the most popular breakfast in Lebanon. Personally, I use naan bread and top it with za'atar and olive oil and bake it for 20 minutes at 350 degrees so I can enjoy the man'ousheh in a short time.

Terms Used in This Book

- "True Parents", "True Father", and "True Mother" refer to Rev. and Mrs. Moon.

- "Brothers" and "Sisters" usually refers to church members.

- "Spiritual Parent" refers to a person who witnesses and brings another person ("spiritual child") to the church.

- "Ambassador for Peace" is a term to refer to a person who actively supports our church values.

www.ingramcontent.com/pod-product-compliance
Lightning Source LLC
Chambersburg PA
CBHW070832160726
48004CB00001B/345